vegan cooking

cooking

IN YOUR

air fryer

vegan cooking
cooking
IN YOUR
air fryer

75 INCREDIBLE
COMFORT FOOD RECIPES WITH
HALF THE CALORIES

kathy hester
**BESTSELLING AUTHOR OF *THE GREAT VEGAN BEAN BOOK* AND
*THE ULTIMATE VEGAN COOKBOOK FOR YOUR INSTANT POT®***

PAGE STREET
PUBLISHING CO.

PAGE STREET
PUBLISHING CO.

First published in 2018 by
Page Street Publishing Co.
27 Congress Street, Suite 105
Salem, MA 01970
www.pagestreetpublishing.com

Distributed by Macmillan, sales in Canada by The Canadian Manda Group.

22 21 20 19 18   1 2 3 4 5

ISBN-13: 978-1-62414-508-7
ISBN-10: 1-62414-508-6

Library of Congress Control Number: 2017952236

Cover and book design by Page Street Publishing Co.

Photography by Kathy Hester

Printed and bound in the United States

  As a member of 1% for the Planet, Page Street Publishing protects our planet by donating to nonprofits like The Trustees, which focuses on local land conservation. Learn more at onepercentfortheplanet.org.

This is dedicated to my beloved cat Irma who passed away in 2016 at 18 years old. She taught me how to be feisty and never give up. This was the first book that I wrote without her by my side. It's hard to believe it, but I missed her interrupting me every few minutes so I could pet her and carry her around.

Contents

Mains: Delightful Dinners That Will Have Your Family Asking for More 89

Side Dishes and Appetizers: Fried Favorites Lightened Up with Air Frying 133

Breakfasts: Easy and Delicious Ways to Start Your Day 165

Desserts: Crispy and Baked Treats That Are Healthier Than You Think 179

Introduction to Your Air Fryer

I'm sure you're going to love your air fryer as much as I do. In this chapter I answer many of your burning questions, plus give you tons of tips and tricks. This is not a chapter you want to skip, so read on!

Why Use an Air Fryer?

When I bought my first air fryer, it was just to play with, but it's quickly become my most-used kitchen appliance. It goes way beyond the typical French fries, fried pickles and onion rings—though it will healthy those up for you too.

The thing I make most in my air fryer is tofu. It makes the tofu so crispy that you might forget you made it with little or no oil. There's a whole section all about tofu on page 22. But don't worry: If you can't eat tofu, there are plenty of things the air fryer can do for you.

Since the air fryer works like a convection oven, you can bake brownies, muffins and even mug cakes in it! Your mug cakes will no longer be a microwaved mess, because the texture will be just right.

It's not limited to sweet items though, and you'll see that in the Vegan Mac and Cheese with a Surprise! (page 103), Stuffed Artichoke with Fresh Herbs (page 156) and Weeknight Calzones (page 99).

Some veggies caramelize a bit in the air fryer, making them addictive. You'll want to try my no-oil Lime Corn on the Cob on page 148 and the Easy Sweet Potato Fries recipe on page 140. Plus, you can roast any vegetables you want in about half the time it would take in a conventional oven.

It makes amazing roasted onions and garlic for spreads and such. Oh, and be prepared to become addicted to the Roasted Tomatillo Green Salsa on page 33.

Air fryers have been available for home use since 2006, but recently they've become more affordable, which means we can all have one now. You may not have heard much about them because they came out in Europe and Asia years before they started promoting them in the United States and Canada.

You may already know me from my blog, HealthySlowCooking.com, or my general obsession with kitchen gadgets, like slow cookers and Instant Pots®. I love it when a simple appliance can help families save money and time all while eating a little bit healthier.

Like everyone else, I started using my air fryer to play with low- and no-oil versions of my favorite fried foods. In no time at all I was heating up frozen "cheater" foods like veggie burgers, frozen tots and fries. Air frying makes these amazing, and I'll talk more about that later on.

For those of you who avoid processed foods, oils or salt, you'll be glad to know that there's a DIY Frozen French Fries recipe in the staples chapter on page 30. With my recipes, you can use a little oil or no oil, whatever fits your eating style, and you can still have the convenience of last-minute fries!

You can air fry using a little bit of oil or even no oil at all. That's how you can easily healthify foods like French fries, chips, onion rings and chicken-fried tofu. With a little oil, these foods are remarkably similar to deep-fried foods with half the calories. Without any oil at all, you'll notice that they do come out a bit drier, but if you already follow a no-oil diet, it's still a healthy way to satisfy some of your cravings.

What the Heck Is an Air Fryer?

An air fryer is actually similar to a convection oven. Warm air is blown all around the food to keep the temperature steady from all directions, similar to the way food is heated during deep-frying. In your air fryer, the heating element is above the food and the fan is above that.

There are three main shapes of air fryers. The first one resembles a countertop deep fryer, only it's a bit bulkier. The second is a large and round one, and it holds more than double the amount of food the others do. Recently, a few convection toaster ovens have added air fry settings, so we have those in the mix too.

There are many different brands, models and sizes of air fryers, and the prices vary accordingly.

Most of the fryers have baskets that look similar to the fry baskets you've seen used in hot oil frying. Your air fryer basket probably has a handle with either a mesh bottom or a nonstick coating with holes to allow the air to circulate evenly. There is even a basket that has a removable top to keep your kale and collard chips from flying up into the heating element.

These baskets are not in the large round ones or the toaster ovens. But, in the ones that have it, there's also a solid pan called a drawer at the bottom, which is there to catch crumbs and drips. The basket goes into the drawer, and then both go in the air fryer together. Both can be removed for cleaning and separated for easier serving. Never try to pour out contents with the basket still attached to the bottom pan!

How Does It Work?

When you add something like potatoes to your air fryer, typically first you'll cook them at a lower temperature to cook the inside of the potato. That way, it won't be burned on the outside before it's done on the inside. Next, you'll crank up the heat and crisp up the outside.

It cooks with radiant heat like your regular oven but adds in a convection fan that makes things cook faster than a typical oven and helps things crisp up.

One of my favorite things is that you can reheat and bake in your air fryer in record time without heating up the whole house. Say hello to quick food all year-round and, as a special bonus, your kitchen will be cooler in the summer too.

Do I Have to Use Oil?

The short answer is no. You can make almost all of the recipes without added oil. The longer answer is that some foods have a better texture when you add a spritz of oil before cooking.

Those of you on no-oil diets will no doubt just be glad to have some crispy, fun food that fits into your diet, and that will be good enough. However, if you are more of a low-oil person, you'll notice that the battered recipes are less dry with a little oil.

I encourage you to experiment within your personal eating rules to find the sweet spot on this. You can also spritz aquafaba (the liquid from a can of cooked chickpeas) or even vegetable broth on to get an in-between effect.

Does All Spray Oil Have Chemical Propellants?

The quick and easy answer is no! It's easier than ever to grab a spray oil that's actually just oil. Just make sure to look at the ingredients, and you'll be able to tell. I've found a variety of oils like canola, olive, avocado and others in places like Whole Foods, chain groceries, Trader Joe's and even at Aldi's.

If there's a specific oil you want to use and you can't find it without chemical propellants, you can use a small spray bottle or a pump bottle made especially to spray oil evenly. Personally, I find that the store-bought bottles do a better job.

Does Food Really Taste the Same as Fried?

Not exactly, because the cooking method is closer to baking. But it goes beyond the almost crispy oven fries you've tried before and have not been happy with. It's a dry method of cooking, so you may notice that battered foods are a little dry. A few spritzes of oil will take care of that.

Food will brown and get crisp and crunchy—plus you can bake normally unfried foods in your air fryer as well. You'll see this with corn on the cob, roasted tomatillo salsa and even dried tomatoes.

How Do I Pick the Right Air Fryer for Me?

Air fryers come in a wide variety of sizes, models and brands, so it can be confusing at first. To make matters worse, some fryers list capacity in quarts and others in pounds.

The first thing to consider is the number of people you regularly cook for, then see what's available in your budget. Air fryer brands and models can vary by more than $100 dollars!

If you cook for only one or two, opt for a smaller (and usually less expensive) model like a GoWISE 3.7 quart. It was my first air fryer and has enough room to cook three veggie burgers. It is often on the cheaper side of air fryers, so that doesn't hurt either. I've used their customer service to get a replacement part, and that went smoothly.

I also have a Phillips Viva, which is close to the same size as my small GoWISE. I got it on super sale at Williams-Sonoma, but it still cost over $100 more than my GoWISE. As I'm writing this book, it is the latest and greatest from Phillips. One of the reasons I wanted to try it was for their improved basket, which has a lid that you can use to keep light foods, like kale or collard chips, from coming in contact with the heating element.

Cooking for Four?

An XL air fryer may fit your needs better. These range from 5 to 6 quarts (4.5 to 5.4 L) or thereabouts. These are more expensive but can often be found on sale at Amazon under their warehouse deals. Many of these were damaged boxes or returns. They will clearly state if they are a refurbished product. For this book, I used the Phillips XL and the GoWISE XL. I got both of these almost half price from Amazon warehouse deals. The Phillips was refurbished and both have worked well.

If you are cooking for a crowd, you may want to get one of the large round ones, which usually hold 10-plus quarts. Some of these are self-stirring, so you don't have to stop and shake when cooking.

Since air fryers are constantly being improved and new models come out frequently, you may want to consult my Facebook Group—Vegan Cooking with Kathy Hester—or my air fryer page at healthyslowcooking.com/airfryers to get the most up-to-date information on particular models.

Where Should My Air Fryer Be When I Cook in It?

Make sure that you are placing your air fryer on a heat-resistant counter with at least 6 inches (15 cm) to a foot (30 cm) of space between the air fryer's exhaust fan and the wall, as well as away from anything that could be melted by hot air.

That means move the bread or any plastic that's nearby, and keep your little ones and four-legged friends away from it.

Do I Really Have to Preheat?

This will have to do with your particular air fryer and should be stated in the manual for your model. Honestly, with the models I have, I almost never preheat.

Some people in the Facebook group Fatfree Vegan Air Fryers (www.facebook.com/groups/FatFreeVeganAF) mention that preheating can help prevent sticking when cooking oil-free.

I find that most newer models don't require preheating. I've baked muffins in the air fryer both ways and didn't see much of a difference. The fact is a convection oven comes up to temperature faster than a conventional oven, and I think it happens even faster in these smaller appliances.

With that said, if your manual says preheat, then I think you should preheat. What the manual says for your particular air fryer is going to be the best way for you to cook in it.

If your air fryer does need preheating, make sure not to add any parchment paper until you add food in the basket to weigh it down or it could fly up into the heater and burn.

Is It Messy to Cook in an Air Fryer?

Most things aren't particularly messy in the air fryer, and I will let you know in the recipes if there's a step that will help make your cleanup easier.

One way to keep your basket looking new is not to spray oil on the food in the basket, but to spray it before you add it to the basket. As with any cooking device, oil can build up on the basket and make it harder to clean. But they cook fine even if they aren't as pretty with a little oil buildup.

If you're picky, you can line your basket with parchment paper, just make sure there is about an inch (2.5 cm) open around the edges of the basket for the air to flow through. You must make sure to have your food on top of the parchment before you do any cooking or it could fly up into the top heating element. Your food will weigh down the parchment and keep it safe.

I go one step further and buy precut round parchment paper that has pre-perforated holes to allow air flow and keep the mess to a minimum. You can buy these in Asian markets or on Amazon—just search for steamer papers.

You can also make your own by buying parchment paper liners for round cake pans. Just fold in half and get busy with your hole puncher.

I've found that even the biggest messes can be cleaned easily since the drawer and baskets usually have nonstick coatings of some kind. All of mine can go in the dishwasher and that helps too.

What about Battered Foods?

Yes, it's still true! In my recipes, when we use a batter, it will then be rolled in breadcrumbs, flour, cornmeal or the like. This will help food to stick together less.

You'll find some recipes online that are just dipped in batter and placed in the basket. I encourage you to line your basket (see Is It Messy to Cook in an Air Fryer? on page 13). You will also need to cook a single layer at a time or the food may stick together. This isn't always a bad thing, and it will still leave you with some crispy coating, though perhaps not all over.

Please note that some of the breading will be blown off by the fan, but there will be enough left to give you a good crunch.

There are a few recipes—like the Southern Air-Fried Hush Puppies on page 143—that can stick a little, especially in the metal mesh baskets. You can always use the modified parchment paper we've talked about.

Also, if you are experimenting with modifying a deep-fat-fried recipe for your air fryer, you should make the coating thicker, and you can always try the first batch in a pan that fits your air fryer as a precaution. Then you'll know if it can go in by itself in the basket or if it needs parchment.

As a final word, I've roasted onions right in the basket, made a burned-on leaky mess, and still had it all clean up fine.

Can I Peek in the Air Fryer to Check on Food?

It's easy to check on your food while it's cooking, and you'll do it more often because many recipes have you shake the basket a few times during cooking. Some models will have a pause button you can use to stop the fans and then restart them again. Other models, like most GoWISE ones, do not have a pause button but will wind down when you remove the basket.

It's not dangerous at all to remove the basket, though at first it seems a little odd to do it. If you are cooking light foods like kale or collard chips, some will fly out if you don't pause it. So if you are using a GoWISE, pull the basket out just enough to stop it, and wait a few seconds for the fan to stop before removing.

I Don't Have a Top Lid. What Can I Do to Secure My Food?

In most recipes you won't need to do anything. But with kale or collard chips, you could get a steamer basket that will fit in your air fryer and act as a protective dome.

If you're toasting a tortilla, you can put a small rack on top. If you have an Instant Pot®, the rack that came with it will probably work. Alternatively, you could buy one specifically for your model of air fryer or pick one up at an Asian market or on Amazon.

What Kinds of Dishes Can I Use?

You can use any oven-safe dish that fits in the size air fryer you have without completely covering all the holes in the basket. You need to make sure the airflow is not compromised.

Ceramics, silicone muffin liners, small pie pans and metal baking dishes all work just fine. You can use oven-safe paper baking molds, but never put plastic in your air fryer.

You can buy dishes made for your air fryer, but most of them are more expensive than small baking dishes and ramekins. I use a 5-inch (13-cm) Wilton cake pan that can be purchased in any craft store will fit in most air fryers and work fine.

As you can see in the photos throughout this book, I have a selection of ceramic dishes that work great too. I get most of these inexpensively at thrift stores.

How Do I Remove Baking Dishes?

Before cooking you can make an aluminum-foil sling by tearing off a piece of foil that will go around the top and bottom of the dish you will be using. Then fold lengthwise in half, then in half again. Place this sling on the counter, then place your dish in the middle. Bring the ends together.

If the dish is heavy, you can make two slings and place them like a cross, then put the dish in the middle and bring up all four to meet. You'll cook with this on; then you can use it to remove the dish using potholders or oven mitts.

You can also use silicone bands that are made in different sizes for this purpose. See the Accessory Resources section on page 193 for more details.

Is It Possible to Cook Prepared Frozen Food in the Air Fryer?

Yes, frozen fries, tots and even vegan "meats" can be cooked in your air fryer. I start these at 390° to 400°F (200° to 205°C) and check every 5 minutes and shake. Some will be done after 10 minutes, and others may take 15 or 20, but if you check every 5 minutes, nothing should burn.

Air Fryer Dos and Don'ts

- Never leave your air fryer unattended while cooking.

- Don't forget the basket bottom is hot and should never be placed directly on a counter after cooking. I put mine on the stovetop or a large trivet.

- Never put anything on the top of your air fryer while it's cooking. Most have vents that need to be clear.

- Don't overfill your air fryer basket or your food won't get as crispy and may take much longer to cook. If your air fryer is small, you may need to cook in multiple batches.

- Unlike with a slow cooker, you can stop and check on your food as often as you'd like.

- Never turn the hot food over with your fingers—always use tongs or pot holders. Remember, it's hot!

- You can use a grate that fits into your air fryer basket to hold down foods while they cook, or use a toothpick to help keep the food where you want it in spite of the strong fan. This is great for taquitos, tacos and even sandwiches.

- Use a spray bottle for oil to get it exactly where you want it and to use less oil.

- Shake the basket often to help foods like chips and fries cook and brown evenly.

- Always remove the air fryer basket from its drawer when serving food.

- Be sure to clean the drawer as well as the basket after each recipe. You can do this in warm, soapy water. Many air fryer baskets and drawers can go into the top shelf of your dishwasher; check your manual to find out if yours can. All of the ones I have can be put in the dishwasher, and it's nice to get them extra clean.

- Don't bother drying the basket—just put it in your air fryer and turn on for a couple of minutes, and it will dry itself!

Why Doesn't My Air Fryer Have the Same Setting for the Temperature in a Recipe?

I can't really tell you why the manufacturers choose to do it differently, but I can tell you that on some the top temperature is 390°F (200°C) and others it's 400°F (205°C). The discrepancies continue from there between makes and models.

Just use the closest setting that your air fryer has. It may be that you cook at 330° to 360°F (166° to 182°C) instead of 350°F (177°C). Just know that if it's a little higher, it should cook a bit faster, so check on it a little earlier than the recipe asks you to.

Remember that some air fryers use manual dials and others digital displays, and, even within a category, they are still not all set to the same temperature.

What Are All Those Buttons?

Again, they change a bit from air fryer to air fryer, but they all have an on/off button and a way to set the temperature, and many have preset cooking cycles for foods like fries.

The best place to get all the information on your particular air fryer is the manual that came with it. I know it's boring, but it will be a quick read. Have you misplaced yours? Look up the make and model online, and I bet you'll find a copy you can download.

Things to Have in Your Air Fryer Pantry

If you are using oil or aquafaba, it's nice to have a few glass spray bottles to spritz battered food. I would recommend also getting a store-bought oil sprayer with no propellants.

For aquafaba, you can use the liquid from a can of cooked chickpeas or the liquid from homemade chickpeas. If your homemade aquafaba is thin, just reduce it in a saucepan until it's thicker. It can be used instead of oil and as an egg substitute.

Breadcrumbs are a must, and that's what gives battered foods the best crunch. You can make your own breadcrumbs by following the super easy recipe on page 29.

When it comes to panko breadcrumbs, you will need to purchase them because they are cooked with an electric current, which is what gives them their special crunch. Panko is lighter, crispier and airier than regular breadcrumbs and absorbs less oil. You can find panko breadcrumbs in whole wheat and gluten-free varieties. I find that panko makes everything crunchier, and it's my favorite type of breadcrumb. If you can't get your hands on any, you can always substitute regular breadcrumbs.

Air Fryer Superpowers

In addition to making healthy "fried" foods without oil, your air fryer can save the day in lots of little time- and space-saving ways.

- Toast bread, bagels or English muffins in it. Try it on 350°F (177°C) and check often depending on how thin your bread is.

- Frozen food can go straight into the air fryer without thawing. This includes things like prepared meals. Cook them on 400°F (205°C) for about 10 minutes. Shake the basket after the first 5 minutes.

- Frozen fries and tots can be cooked on 400°F (205°C) for about 10 minutes.

- Frozen veggie burgers work great on 375°F (191°C) for 15 minutes.

- Reheat leftover pizza or any leftovers in your air fryer on 350°F (177°C) until piping hot.

- Use it like a mini oven during the summer to keep your house cooler. It can also be used as an extra oven for big holiday gatherings.

- Toast nuts, croutons, etc. in less time right in your air fryer.

- You can also do some dehydration, but only very small batches. Check out the recipe for Air Fryer Dried Tomatoes on page 53.

- Remember, you can make fries and chips out of any root vegetable. It's a great way to use up that rutabaga that comes in your winter community farm box.

- When you start experimenting with your own recipes, try starting at 350°F (177°C) for 5 minutes at a time until done. If you want something extra crispy, do the last few minutes at 400°F (205°C).

Where Can I Get Accessories and Baking Dishes That Fit My Air Fryer?

For most cooking, you'll use the basket as is, but to cook patties or particularly wet items you will place a piece of parchment paper in the basket. It's important that the paper doesn't cover the whole basket, so leave open about 1 inch (2.5 cm) between the sides of the basket and the paper.

You can also bake in your air fryer using any oven-safe dish that will comfortably fit in the basket while leaving about an inch (2.5 cm) around for the air to circulate. That means that you can make mug cakes without using a microwave, and prepare just enough of your favorite casseroles for dinner for one night.

You can get accessories from your air fryer manufacturer, Amazon, craft stores, thrift stores, etc. Just make sure that they fit in your air fryer without covering up all the holes in the basket and are oven safe.

Special Diet Considerations

If you have any of my other cookbooks, or read my blog HealthySlowCooking.com, you know that I do my best to make options in my recipes so everyone can enjoy them.

Low or No Salt

In most of the recipes, I ask that you add salt to taste. If a recipe calls for a certain amount of salt, it's because it needs extra seasoning or salt needs to be added before the end.

Feel free to substitute your favorite salt-free herb blend, or just increase the seasonings in those recipes and leave out the salt.

No Added Oil

If you are on a no-oil diet, you will be able to make all of the recipes with a few adjustments. While I offer the option to use a small amount of oil or spray oil, you can always use aquafaba to get the spices and coatings to stick to your food.

Gluten-Free

If you are gluten-free due to celiac disease or allergies, always check labels on grains, sauces and the like for a clear statement that the product is gluten-free. Remember that some grains, like oats, are often contaminated with other gluten-containing food products, but there are places like Bob's Red Mill that have dedicated allergy-free production facilities.

You can use a gluten-free baking mix as a replacement for whole wheat pastry flour, spelt flour, etc. This is what I do in my own kitchen when I bake gluten-free.

Soy-Free

I've tried to provide substitutes or alternatives to soy products when used. You can use hemp tofu or hemp tempeh in many of the recipes in place of soy tofu, and use almond or coconut milk in place of soy yogurt.

You can also substitute seitan, jackfruit and even chickpeas in many recipes that call for tofu. If you use chickpeas, you will want to cut the cooking time in half or add them in toward the end of the recipe cook time unless you want them extra crunchy!

Nutritional Information Disclaimer

Nutritional information is included in this book to give a ballpark idea on calories and the like. All of the recipes have many options that could change the numbers drastically. If you have a medical condition that requires you to keep close track of those numbers, please enter the exact amount and ingredients that you are using into your doctor's recommended nutritional tracker. Some recipes do not include nutritional data because there are too many variables; these recipes are noted.

Make It Yourself

Staples You Will Use Again and Again

If you have any of my other cookbooks, you know I always try to give you all the options you need to make things from scratch. I know many of you prefer not to buy premade staples, but if that's not you, please use store-bought in the recipes to save you time.

In this chapter you'll find spice blends, tips on French fries, tofu and aquafaba. There are also recipes to make your own tomato powder from cherry tomatoes you dry right in your air fryer. Make tomatillo sauce from scratch in minutes and oh so much more!

Aquafaba

GLUTEN-FREE, SOY-FREE, NO OIL ADDED

Aquafaba is the new vegan "it" item, and it's great for air frying. It works in place of oil and even takes the place of egg in batters. There are 2 ways to get aquafaba. The first, and easiest, is to drain the liquid from any size can of cooked chickpeas and save it for a few days in the refrigerator.

The second way is more budget-friendly than buying precooked chickpeas. Just save your cooking liquid when you make homemade chickpeas. If you're like me, you may end up with thin liquid, and then you'll need to do one more step. Simmer the liquid in an uncovered pan until it's reduced by one-third to half or begins to have a consistency more like egg whites.

NOTES: No nutritional data is provided for this recipe because it depends on how thick it is and if anything is added to the beans when cooking.

You can use other bean-cooking liquids as well, but some seem to work a little better than others.

Talking Tofu

GLUTEN-FREE, NO OIL ADDED OPTION

Of all the things I make in the air fryer, tofu is my favorite. Air frying makes it crispy and delicious.

What type of tofu works?

Really just about any type other than soft or silken tofu. I've started buying extra-firm, high-protein tofu so I can skip pressing it. All you need to do is cut and go.

How do I press tofu?

You can use a fancy gadget called a tofu press—it's amazing but a little pricey. You don't have to spend any money though—just use heavy things that are already in your kitchen.

The reason we press tofu is to get the water out. That makes for a crispy fried tofu and creates space for the tofu to soak up a marinade.

Wrap the tofu in clean kitchen towels or paper towels and place it on a cutting board. I take a cast-iron skillet and place it on top of that, balanced with a bag of flour. You can use any pan and as much weight as it will hold. Be mindful that the things you pile up could fall, so be sure to push it toward the back of your counter. That way if it all falls, it won't hit your foot, dog or child.

Do I need to use oil?

No. Sometimes I do, and sometimes I don't. Plus, aquafaba is always an oil-free option.

What do I use to coat it?

If you are using a recipe, it will tell you. If you are experimenting, you can use any of the following: cornstarch, potato starch, tapioca starch, wheat flour, rice flour, chickpea flour, cornmeal, breadcrumbs, herbs or minced nuts.

If your tofu is still a little wet, the flour or spices may stick on it as is, without additional oil. If not, a little spritz of oil or aquafaba will help.

How long do I cook it?

It depends on the size of the pieces and the size of your air fryer. As you experiment, start at 375°F (190°C) and cook 5 minutes at a time, and repeat until it's crisp and brown.

NOTE: Many people like to freeze tofu to give it a denser and meatier consistency. Just pop the whole, unopened container into your freezer. Thaw overnight in the fridge, squeeze the water out with your hands and then follow the recipe. Do not do this with silken tofu!

Everything You Need to Know about French Fries

I know one of the first things that you'll want to make is French fries. The air fryer makes amazing fries, but they do take some planning. If you aren't a planner, go ahead and skip to the DIY Frozen Fries recipe on page 30. That way you can make them quickly and have only what you want in them.

What kind of potatoes work best?

Honestly, I use whatever I have on hand, but you can't go wrong with a nice large Idaho russet potato.

Should I peel them?

If they aren't organic, I suggest you peel them. But if they are organic, the skins can add some color, especially if you are using red- or purple-skinned potatoes.

How should I cut them?

You can freehand slice them with a sharp knife, use a julienne setting on your mandoline, buy a French fry cutter or make super thin ones on a spiralizer. Just remember that the smaller or thinner you cut them, the less time you'll cook them, and if they are large or thick, you may need to add extra time.

Why soak and then dry the fries?

I know, it's a pain, and that's the main reason I like to do a big batch to freeze all at once. It does make a difference in crispiness, so it is well worth doing. It removes some of the natural starch, making them crispier and helping them not to stick together.

Some people soak for as little as 20 minutes and up to 8 or 9 hours. Whenever possible, I like to throw them in the water and place in the fridge for about 6 hours, but any time will help.

Traditionally the fries are dried after soaking so as not to react to the oil. We do that for the air fryer to make them crisp up better.

Oil or no oil?

That is all up to you. I usually spray a little olive oil on mine, but aquafaba works just as well. Both will help salt and any seasoning mix you use stick to the fries through cooking.

How do I air fry them after all that?

Since you are working with raw potatoes and not blanched ones, you are going to cook them at two different temperatures, the first to cook the inside of the potato, and the second to crisp them up. I cook at 330°F (166°C) until the potatoes are soft, about 20 to 30 minutes depending on thickness, then I crisp up the outsides at 400°F (205°C) for about 10 minutes until browned and crisp. Timing varies according to the size of the fries.

What if I really need some homemade fries sooner than that?

Then you can blanch the fries in boiling water.

Bring a pot of water to boil, place the fries in and cook until almost tender, but not so much that the potatoes are soft enough to break. I do this for about 5 minutes for medium-size fries.

Drain them in a colander and dry on clean kitchen towels or paper towels. Toss in oil or aquafaba, add seasonings and/or salt, then air fry at 400°F (205°C) until browned and crispy.

Ketchup or vegan mayo?

My answer is both. Don't forget you can make your own flavored ketchup by adding a little hot sauce, liquid smoke or a spice blend. You can do the same with mayo, and sriracha mayo is a killer sandwich spread too.

NOTE: No nutritionals are provided for this recipe because they depend on how thick the fries are and if anything is added to the fries when cooking.

Basic Whole Wheat Bread Dough

SOY-FREE, NO OIL ADDED

There's something so satisfying about making recipes with homemade bread dough. This bread is easy to make, and you can use it from the fridge for 5 days or the freezer for up to 3 months. You'll use this in the Weeknight Calzones recipe on page 99, the Date-Caramel Pecan Rolls recipe on page 177 and the Garlic Breadsticks on page 160.

MAKES 4 RECIPES' WORTH OF DOUGH

2 cups (473 ml) warm water

1 tbsp (19 g) sugar, agave or maple syrup

1 tbsp (9 g) baking yeast

2 tbsp (30 ml) aquafaba

3 cups (360 g) whole wheat flour

2 cups (226 g) white whole wheat flour (or use regular whole wheat flour)

2 tsp (4 g) salt

NOTES: You can freeze them all, but I can't resist making a recipe my family can eat!

Are you gluten-free? Then just substitute your favorite gluten-free pizza dough in the recipes that call for this.

Add the warm water, sugar and yeast to the bowl of your mixer. Let sit 10 minutes or until it begins to foam. If your yeast doesn't foam at all, your yeast may be out of date and won't make your bread rise.

Once foamy, add the aquafaba (or use a mild oil if you prefer) and mix.

Combine the flours and salt in a mixing bowl and mix well. Add the flour 1 cup (120 g) at a time to the yeast mixture in the mixer. Mix using the paddle attachment until the dough begins to get too thick, and then change to the dough hook.

Finish adding in the flour mixture until the dough is no longer sticky, but not too dry. Knead for 10 minutes.

No mixer? No problem! Just mix everything as above in a mixing bowl. Use a spoon until the dough is too thick, then scrape out the dough onto a floured cutting board. Instead of kneading 10 minutes, it will probably take 20 minutes. You'll know you're done kneading because the dough will feel like the bottom of your earlobe.

Divide the dough into 4 pieces. Use one piece now and put the rest in the fridge for 4 to 5 days, or freeze and thaw to use later.

AMOUNT PER SERVING: 1 piece of dough · CALORIES: 552.8 · TOTAL FAT: 2.0 g · SODIUM: 1,166.9 mg · TOTAL CARBS: 109.9 g · DIETARY FIBER: 9.1 g · PROTEIN: 18.3 g

DIY Breadcrumbs

GLUTEN-FREE OPTION*, SOY-FREE OPTION*, NO OIL ADDED OPTION*

There's no need to buy expensive, premade breadcrumbs when all you need is some stale, or even fresh, bread. If you want to make it seasoned, just add seasonings in. One of my favorites is to add a tablespoon or two of Italian Seasoning Blend (see recipe on page 58). You can use these in any recipe that calls for breadcrumbs. Just know that regular breadcrumbs are not as crispy as panko breadcrumbs, which you have to buy.

MAKES 1 TO 2 CUPS (100 TO 200 G), DEPENDING ON THE SIZE OF YOUR BREAD SLICES

4 slices of bread (*selected without the ingredients that you are avoiding), cut into cubes

Place the bread in your air fryer. Set your air fryer to 350°F (177°C) and set the timer for 3 minutes. Flip the bread and cook for 3 minutes more. Repeat if the bread is still very moist.

Let cool, then crumble with your hands, a potato masher or in your food processor. A food processor will make fine, consistent crumbs, and the other two methods will yield more rustic breadcrumbs.

NOTE: No nutritionals are provided for this recipe because they depend on the type of bread you use.

DIY Frozen French Fries

GLUTEN-FREE, SOY-FREE, NO OIL ADDED

We all love French fries, but I don't like how long you have to wait for them to soak and dry before you air fry them. It's just too long when I'm making a last-minute dinner. One solution is to buy frozen fries, but they often have ingredients I don't want, and they certainly aren't salt- or oil-free. My solution is to make your own frozen fries, and you get to choose exactly what you want in them. I get a giant bag of potatoes at Costco and spend a day every few months stocking the freezer with them.

MAKES 4 SERVINGS

1 tsp (2 g) salt (optional)

4 large russet potatoes (900 g), cut into fry shapes

Spray oil (optional)

NOTES: Make a batch every month or make a triple batch a few times a year. They will keep frozen for up to 4 months.

If your family loves fries as much as mine does, you might want to get an inexpensive fry cutter. It makes all the fries the same size and makes them cook more evenly.

Bring a stockpot half full of water and salt, if using, to a boil. Add one-fourth to half of your cut potatoes to the boiling water and cook for 5 minutes.

Have an ice bath ready in a heatproof bowl. Using a slotted spoon or scoop, remove the boiled fries and place in the ice bath. Repeat with the remaining potatoes.

Place a double layer of paper towels on a large baking sheet, and place the cooled fries in a single layer. I also cover the top of them with a single layer of paper towels to dry the tops. Let dry.

If you want, you can transfer the fries to a bowl and toss with spray oil.

Remove the paper towels and once again arrange the fries in a single layer on the baking sheet, and place in your freezer for 1 hour. By freezing them separately first, then putting them in a resealable freezer bag, they won't freeze into a big clump, and you can remove just what you need.

HOW TO COOK YOUR FROZEN FRIES

Cook at 400°F (205°C) for 10 minutes, shake and cook 5 minutes more. Shake one more time and cook 5 more minutes or until brown and crispy.

AMOUNT PER SERVING: Fries from 1 potato • CALORIES: 255.9 • TOTAL FAT: 0.3 g • SODIUM: 640.1 mg • TOTAL CARBS: 58.0 g • DIETARY FIBER: 8.8 g • PROTEIN: 6.2 g

Roasted Tomatillo Green Salsa

There is no flavor match to the tanginess of tomatillos. They look like little green tomatoes covered in a husk, but they have a flair of their own. Once you try this roasted tomatillo salsa, you'll never buy store-bought again. It's ridiculously easy, and you can adjust the heat to suit your family's taste.

MAKES ABOUT 1 CUP (240 ML)

4 large tomatillos, cut into sixths (about 2 cups [264 g])

½ cup (71 g) onion slices

1 small (14 g) seeded jalapeño, cut in half (or more if you like it extra spicy)

3 whole cloves (9 g) garlic

2 tsp (10 ml) lime juice

½ tsp salt, or to taste

¼ cup (4 g) minced cilantro

Add the tomatillos, onion and jalapeño to your air fryer basket and cook at 390°F (200°C) for 10 minutes.

Add the garlic and roast 3 more minutes.

Place the roasted veggies in your blender or food processor with the lime juice and salt. Blend until smooth in the blender, or use your food processor to make it a little chunky.

Pour the mixture in a bowl and fold in the minced cilantro. If you are a cilantro hater, just leave it out!

NOTE: Use this on any Mexican food that you love. It's great on the Black Bean Avocado Chimichangas on page 131 and the Air-Fried Pupusas on page 117. If you have a Hispanic market in your area, that's where you will find lots of bargain-friendly veggies—especially tomatillos, fresh and dried chile peppers and the freshest masa.

AMOUNT PER SERVING: 2 tbsp (31 g) · CALORIES: 10.7 · TOTAL FAT: 0.2 g · SODIUM: 0.6 mg · TOTAL CARBS: 2.1 g · DIETARY FIBER: 0.5 g · PROTEIN: 0.3 g

Ranch Dressing

GLUTEN-FREE, SOY-FREE OPTION*, NO OIL ADDED

Everyone needs a good ranch dressing in their repertoire, and this one couldn't be easier! The base is vegan yogurt, and I love soy yogurt for this, but there are plenty of new unsweetened almond and cashew vegan yogurts around now too. This is a must-have dip for the Buttermilk-Style Fried Pickles on page 144 and it's my favorite on the Battered Onion Rings on page 139.

MAKES ABOUT 1½ CUPS (360 ML)

¾ cup (177 ml) soy milk mixed with 1 tbsp (15 ml) apple cider vinegar (*use other nondairy milk)

½ cup (113 g) unsweetened plain vegan yogurt

1¼ tsp (3 g) granulated garlic

1½ tsp (3 g) salt

¾ tsp onion powder

½ tsp dill

¼ tsp black pepper

Whisk all the ingredients together. Store in the refrigerator. Use as a dip or salad dressing.

AMOUNT PER SERVING: 2 tbsp (30 ml) • CALORIES: 15.7 • TOTAL FAT: 0.8 g • CHOLESTEROL: 0.0 mg • SODIUM: 457.5 mg • TOTAL CARBS: 2.4 g • DIETARY FIBER: 0.6 g • PROTEIN: 0.6 g

Extra-Tangy Cashew Cheese

GLUTEN-FREE, SOY-FREE, NO OIL ADDED

This is an easy-to-make thick, spreadable vegan cheese. The tang it gets from the apple cider vinegar reminds me of goat cheese, a flavor that isn't easily found in store-bought vegan cheeses. You can flavor it with cracked black pepper, fresh herbs or your favorite flavors.

MAKES ABOUT 1¼ CUPS (ABOUT 280 G)

1 cup (113 g) raw cashew pieces, soaked for at least 2 hours

3 tbsp (45 ml) unsweetened nondairy milk, or more as needed

1 tbsp (15 ml) apple cider vinegar

2 tsp (3 g) nutritional yeast

½ tsp salt, or to taste

OPTIONAL FLAVORINGS

⅓ tsp minced fresh rosemary

1 tbsp (9 g) minced dried figs and 1 tsp (5 ml) agave nectar or maple syrup

1 tsp (2 g) each fresh minced parsley, basil and oregano

2 tbsp (14 g) minced dried cranberries

Add the soaked cashews, nondairy milk, vinegar, nutritional yeast and salt to your blender and blend until smooth. You may need to scrape the sides down a few times and add extra nondairy milk 1 tablespoon (15 ml) at a time until it's smooth.

You can either leave it plain or add one or more of the optional flavors listed in the ingredients and mix well.

Store in the fridge for up to a week.

NOTE: This is great in the Weeknight Calzones on page 99 and really makes the Fried Green Olives on page 163 an appetizer to remember.

AMOUNT PER SERVING: 2 tbsp (30 g) • CALORIES: 74.0 • TOTAL FAT: 5.7 g • SODIUM: 119.3 mg • TOTAL CARBS: 3.4 g • DIETARY FIBER: 0.9 • PROTEIN: 2.2 g

Roasted Garlic

GLUTEN-FREE, SOY-FREE, NO OIL ADDED OPTION*

Roasted garlic is such a simple thing, but it turns everything it touches to deliciousness. You can use this in the Garlic Breadsticks on page 160, in Weeknight Calzones on page 99 and be sure to try it in your next homemade salad dressing too!

MAKES 1 HEAD (BUT YOU CAN DOUBLE, TRIPLE OR EVEN QUADRUPLE THE RECIPE!)

1 head (6 g) whole garlic

1–2 tsp (5–10 ml) olive oil (*omit)

Cut the top third off of the garlic head (that's the thinner part that comes to a point).

Place in aluminum foil or an oven-safe pan with a lid and drizzle with olive oil, if using. Close the foil tightly or cover with the oven-safe lid.

Add the prepared garlic to your air fryer basket and cook at 400°F (205°C) for 30 minutes or until the garlic is soft and slightly caramelized.

Squeeze the cloves out and store in the fridge for up to a week. Use it to make the oil-free garlic spread on page 160, and use on pizzas, pastas, calzones and anywhere else you want a flavor burst.

You can freeze leftover roasted cloves for later!

NOTES: I did an extra 10 minutes when I cooked 2 heads at once.

You don't have to cook just one head of garlic at a time. Make as many as will fit in your air fryer, and use aluminum foil or a larger oven-safe pan with a lid. Fit as many as you can in a single layer. You may need to cook a bit longer, so keep checking every 10 minutes.

AMOUNT PER SERVING: 1 clove · CALORIES: 13.2 · TOTAL FAT: 0.9 g · SODIUM: 0.8 mg · TOTAL CARBS: 1.2 g · DIETARY FIBER: 0.1 g · PROTEIN: 0.2 g

Cauliflower Chorizo

GLUTEN-FREE, SOY-FREE, NO OIL ADDED

It can be hard to find vegan chorizo that's soy-free and gluten-free, so I wanted to share this homemade version with you. As written it uses cauliflower, but you can sub pressed crumbled tofu or any veggie that can be riced in your food processor. Try this in the Air-Fried Pupusas on page 117.

MAKES ABOUT 2 CUPS (214 G)

4 cups (428 g) cauliflower florets

I tbsp (7 g) Chorizo Spice Blend (page 62)

Salt to taste (optional)

Roast the cauliflower in your air fryer at 350°F (177°C) for 5 minutes. Pour into your food processor with the Chorizo Spice Blend and salt, if using. Pulse until the cauliflower looks like rice or couscous, small bits.

Store in the fridge for up to 3 days, or freeze for up to 2 months.

NOTES: If you don't feel like making your own Chorizo Spice Blend, you can buy premade online at Penzeys or Savory Spice Shop.

Go chorizo crazy and try making it out of pressed crumbled tofu, crumbled tempeh or other veggies that can be "riced," like broccoli and carrots.

SERVINGS PER RECIPE: 4 • AMOUNT PER SERVING: ½ cup (54 g) • CALORIES: 20.0 • TOTAL FAT: 0.0 g • CHOLESTEROL: 0.0 mg • SODIUM: 25.0 mg • TOTAL CARBS: 3.0 g • DIETARY FIBER: 2.0 g • PROTEIN: 2.0 g

Easy DIY Seitan Rolls

SOY-FREE, NO OIL ADDED

Seitan is really easy to make, and you can freeze leftovers for a meal another time. I use this in the Air-Fried Seitan and Veggies with Peanut Sauce on page 104. I also like to use a mandoline to slice it thin for sandwiches. Serve it warm over toast with gravy, and you'll be surprised at the memories it pulls up!

MAKES 2 SEITAN ROLLS, SERVES 8 EACH

1 (15-oz [425-g]) can chickpeas, drained (save liquid for aquafaba)

1½ cups (375 ml) water

¼ cup + 2 tbsp (40 g) nutritional yeast

1 tsp (2 g) salt

1 tbsp (15 g) tomato paste

½ tsp minced garlic

½ tsp dried marjoram

½ tsp dried thyme

⅛ tsp rosemary powder (or ¼ tsp dried rosemary)

1½ cups (216 g) vital wheat gluten flour

Add the chickpeas, water, nutritional yeast, salt, tomato paste, garlic, marjoram, thyme and rosemary into your blender and blend until smooth.

Add the vital wheat gluten flour to a mixing bowl and mix in the chickpea liquid mixture. Knead until smooth and elastic.

Divide the dough into 2 pieces. Place on a piece of parchment paper and roll each dough piece into a log form, and then roll that up in aluminum foil and twist the ends closed. Place both wrapped logs into your air fryer basket.

Bake at 330°F (166°C) for 40 minutes. Cook for 20 minutes more, check one for doneness (cut in half) and wrap back up and cook more if needed. The crust will be a bit tougher than steamed seitan.

Store in the fridge or freeze for later. If you choose to freeze it, cut it first to make it easier to use when you're ready for it.

NOTES: I like to use a mandoline and thinly slice half a roll. This is great for a homemade sandwich, and I love to warm it up and serve it over toast, mashed potatoes or steamed rice and top with gravy. It's the perfect comfort food. You could also shred some with the largest hole on your grater.

You can cut half up in chunks and use in place of tofu, soy curls or tempeh in any recipe.

NOTES: If you have one, you can use a stand mixer to knead instead. Just use the paddle attachment, and let it knead the dough for 5 minutes.

As long as you can eat gluten, I recommend making a batch about once a month. With the 2 rolls you can make about 4 meals for 4.

AMOUNT PER SERVING: ¹⁄₁₆ of a recipe or ⅛ of one roll • CALORIES: 194.1 • TOTAL FAT: 1.5 g • SODIUM: 495.5 mg • TOTAL CARBS: 21.4 g • DIETARY FIBER: 4.2 g • PROTEIN: 25.6 g

Cilantro Mint Chutney

GLUTEN-FREE, SOY-FREE, NO OIL ADDED

This is a beautiful green sauce, and you can make it thicker by adding more herbs and thinner by adding a little more water. This Indian chutney is a must on the Samosa Chaat on page 93 and is a great dip for the Indian-Inspired Veggie Tots on page 136.

MAKES ABOUT 2 CUPS (80 G)

1 cup (about 16 g) fresh cilantro

1 cup (about 30 g) fresh mint

1 tbsp (15 ml) lemon juice

¼ tsp salt

Up to ¼ cup (60 ml) water

Add the cilantro, mint, lemon juice and salt to your blender or small food processor. You will find the mixture is too dry to puree properly, so add the water 1 tablespoon (15 ml) at a time until it can blend smoothly.

NOTE: If you have a large blender, you might want to double the recipe to get it to blend well, or you could make it in a small food processor.

AMOUNT PER SERVING: ½ cup (20 g) • CALORIES: 11.0 •
TOTAL FAT: 0.0 g • SODIUM: 73.7 mg • TOTAL CARBS: 0.2 g •
DIETARY FIBER: 0.0 g • PROTEIN: 0.0 g

Tamarind Chutney

GLUTEN-FREE, SOY-FREE, NO OIL ADDED

This is my favorite Indian dipping sauce. It's sweet, tangy and slightly tart. It's amazing on the Samosa Chaat on page 93 and a great dipping sauce for the Indian-Inspired Veggie Tots on page 136.

MAKES ABOUT 1 CUP (240 ML)

1 cup (237 ml) water

1 cup (200 g) vegan sugar or jaggery

2 tbsp (30 g) tamarind concentrate

Add all the ingredients to a saucepan and bring to a boil. Then turn heat to low and simmer until the mixture has reduced to 1 cup (240 ml) and is thick.

NOTE: You can find tamarind concentrate in your local Indian store or online.

AMOUNT PER SERVING: ¼ cup (60 ml) • CALORIES: 240.0 • TOTAL FAT: 0.0 g • SODIUM: 0.0 mg • TOTAL CARBS: 62.5 g • DIETARY FIBER: 0.0 g • PROTEIN: 0 g

Easy Pineapple Teriyaki Sauce

GLUTEN-FREE OPTION*, SOY-FREE OPTION**, NO OIL ADDED

I have to admit before I made this recipe I often bought premade teriyaki sauce. It's not inexpensive, but it makes a quick stir-fry into a reason to never get takeout again. You do have to cook the homemade version on the stove for a bit, but you can make a double or triple batch at a time and freeze in ice cube trays for a last-minute meal. You can use this on the Teriyaki Soy Curl Dinner recipe on page 100.

MAKES ABOUT 1½ CUPS (360 ML)

2 cups (330 g) minced pineapple (fresh or canned)

⅓ cup (80 g) soy sauce (*use gluten-free or **coconut aminos)

2 tbsp (30 g) coconut or brown sugar (or sweetener of choice, to taste)

1 tbsp (15 ml) rice wine vinegar

1 tbsp (6 g) minced ginger

2 tsp (5 g) minced garlic

Add all the ingredients to a saucepan, and cook over high heat until it just begins to bubble. Turn the heat to low and simmer for 5 minutes.

Carefully transfer the hot sauce to your blender and blend until smooth.

NOTE: This sauce can be used as a dipping sauce for plain fried tofu or roasted veggies, so you may want to keep some in your freezer for a last-minute treat.

AMOUNT PER SERVING: ½ cup (120 ml) · CALORIES: 57.9 · TOTAL FAT: 0.5 g · SODIUM: 951.4 mg · TOTAL CARBS: 14.6 g · DIETARY FIBER: 0.9 g · PROTEIN: 1.3 g

Savory Onion Cream

GLUTEN-FREE, SOY-FREE, NO OIL ADDED

This flavorful sauce is a great way to create cream soups and sauces. Mix in a teaspoon or two (5 to 10 ml) of lemon juice or apple cider vinegar and top your burritos or tacos. You can even just blend it as is with the Roasted Tomatillo Green Salsa (page 33) to make a creamy sauce for the Air-Fried Pupusas on page 117.

MAKES ABOUT 1 CUP (228 G)

1 large (150 g) onion (but not so large that it can't fit in your air fryer whole) or 3 small onions

½ tsp salt, or to taste

Set the whole, unpeeled onion in a baking dish with an onion-size piece of parchment paper in it for easy cleanup. (Do not put directly in your air fryer basket, because it will be a mess to clean up!)

Cook on 400°F (205°C) for 25 minutes, check and cook 20 minutes more. Carefully remove the pan and let the onion cool.

Once cool, peel the skin off, remove any dark or burned parts of the flesh and remove the ends.

Cut in half and put the pieces into your blender with salt.

Store in the refrigerator for up to 4 days.

> **NOTE:** This onion cream is used in the Vegan Mac and Cheese with a Surprise! recipe on page 103. Use this when you'd like a creamy texture with no fat, or as a sour cream substitute.

AMOUNT PER SERVING: ¼ cup (about 57 g) · CALORIES: 14.3 · TOTAL FAT: 0.1 g · SODIUM: 291.8 mg · TOTAL CARBS: 3.2 g · DIETARY FIBER: 0.7 g · PROTEIN: 0.4 g

Air Fryer Dried Tomatoes

GLUTEN-FREE, SOY-FREE, NO OIL ADDED

This is when you realize there's another side to your air fryer. It's so much more than a fry maker. You can even dehydrate small batches of veggies in it! I love making my own dried tomatoes and you will too.

MAKES ABOUT 1 PINT (170 G)

1 pint (280–310 g) cherry or grape tomatoes, halved lengthwise

Place the tomato halves cut-side up in your air fryer basket. Cook on 150°F (66°C) for 1 hour. Check, then cook again for 1 hour.

The tomato halves should be dry enough to shake now but will still need to dry out more to store them, so shake and cook 1 hour more.

Shake again and check for doneness. If you are using in a cooked dish, they can be a little soft, but if you're using them in the DIY Tomato Powder on page 61, they need to be bone dry, so you will cook an additional 30 minutes to 1 hour more.

Store in an airtight container.

NOTE: We will use these (or store-bought dried tomatoes) to make the DIY Tomato Powder on page 61. Then the tomato powder goes into the Homemade BBQ Seasoning Blend on page 57, which makes a mean chip seasoning!

AMOUNT PER SERVING: ¼ pint (48 g) · CALORIES: 43.2 · TOTAL FAT: 0.5 g · SODIUM: 11.2 mg · TOTAL CARBS: 9.6 g · DIETARY FIBER: 3.2 g · PROTEIN: 1.6 g

Homemade Spice Blends

I love to make my own spice blends. It allows me to tailor them to my family's tastes and often costs less than buying fancy premade blends. Once you start, you might just get addicted to making them like I have.

NOTE: None of the spice blends will have nutritional data.

Dill Seasoning Blend

GLUTEN-FREE, SOY-FREE, NO OIL ADDED

There's no combination that goes together like dill and beets. This Dill Seasoning Blend is amazing on beets, both roasted and air fried into thin Dill Beet Chips as in the recipe on page 78.

MAKES ABOUT ¼ CUP (ABOUT 30 G)

2 tbsp (6 g) dried dill

2 tsp (5 g) granulated garlic powder

1½ tsp (7 g) onion powder

½–¾ tsp salt (optional) (or to taste)

½ tsp black pepper

Add all the ingredients to a small container that has a tightly fitting lid. Shake well and stir with a spoon, if needed, to mix well. Store in an airtight container.

Homemade BBQ Seasoning Blend

GLUTEN-FREE, SOY-FREE, NO OIL ADDED

BBQ was my favorite potato chip flavor growing up. Of course, there were tons of things in those that I avoid now. However, you can make a homemade seasoning mix and tailor it to your specific diet! Then sprinkle on Air Fryer Potato Chips (see page 77) or anything else where you want a flavor blast of smoky, sweet, tomato goodness.

> **MAKES ABOUT ¼ CUP (ABOUT 30 G)**

1 tbsp + 2 tsp (12 g) smoked paprika

1 tbsp (7 g) onion powder

2 tsp (4 g) salt (optional)

2 tsp (5 g) tomato powder (optional)

2 tsp (8 g) coconut or vegan sugar (optional)

2 tsp (6 g) granulated garlic powder

1½ tsp (4 g) chili powder blend

½ tsp dry mustard

½ tsp black pepper

Add all the ingredients to your dry blender (be sure there's no water at all or you will make a paste instead of a powder). Cover tightly and blend until smooth. Let the powder settle before you open it or you will breathe it all in.

Store in an airtight container.

Italian Seasoning Blend

GLUTEN-FREE, SOY-FREE, NO OIL ADDED

When I call for Italian seasoning in my recipes, this is what I'm using. If you already have a favorite blend, feel free to keep using it, but if you don't, maybe you'll love this one as much as I do! This recipe is used on the Bow Tie Pasta Chips on page 81, but be sure to mix some into a batch of DIY Breadcrumbs (page 29) too.

MAKES ABOUT ¼ CUP (ABOUT 30 G)

1 tbsp (5 g) dried basil

1 tbsp (5 g) dried oregano

1 tbsp (2 g) dried marjoram

1 tbsp (4 g) dried thyme

1 tsp (7 g) dried rosemary or ½ tsp ground

Add everything to a food processor and process until uniform. Store in an airtight jar.

DIY Tomato Powder

GLUTEN-FREE, SOY-FREE, NO OIL ADDED

Tomato powder packs a big flavor punch and is great in seasoning blends, soups and stews. Unfortunately, it can be hard to find. But all you need is some dried tomatoes and a blender to make your own. This goes into the Homemade BBQ Seasoning Blend on page 57.

MAKES ABOUT ¼ CUP (ABOUT 30 G)

1 cup (120 g) dried tomatoes (NOT oil-packed)

If your tomatoes are not bone dry, toss them into your air fryer for about 3 to 5 minutes to crisp them up. If they are moist, they will not blend into a powder.

If they are bone dry, just toss into your blender and blend until powdered.

Be sure to let the dust settle for a few minutes before you open the blender lid or you'll be breathing in the powder.

Store in an airtight container, and I suggest that you toss in a silica packet from your vitamins to help it stay dry.

DIY Chile Powder Blend

GLUTEN-FREE, SOY-FREE, NO OIL ADDED

I often buy my chile powder from Rancho Gordo, but it's not that hard to make it at home, so why not try it? The best place to get dried chiles is your local Hispanic grocery. They are so cheap compared to regular stores and usually much fresher too.

MAKES ABOUT ¼ CUP (ABOUT 30 G), DEPENDING ON THE SIZE OF YOUR DRIED PEPPERS

7 dried guajillo chile peppers

4 dried cascabel chile peppers

3 dried ancho chile peppers

2 dried New Mexico chile peppers

Toast the chiles in your air fryer at 380°F (193°C) for 2 minutes or until fragrant and brittle.

Let cool, then remove stems (and seeds if you'd like). Blend in a blender until it's a powder.

Chorizo Spice Blend

GLUTEN-FREE, SOY-FREE, NO OIL ADDED

This blend is mild while giving a ton of roasted chile flavor. Make it spicy by adding a teaspoon (2 g) of habanero or cayenne pepper powder. This is used in the Cauliflower Chorizo on page 41.

MAKES ½ CUP (ABOUT 60 G)

3 tbsp (21 g) chili powder or DIY Chile Powder Blend (above)

1 tbsp + 1 tsp (9 g) ground cumin

1 tbsp + 1 tsp (9 g) granulated garlic

1½ tsp (3 g) ground coriander

1 tsp (2 g) dried oregano

1 tsp (2 g) dried thyme

¾ tsp ground black pepper

¼ tsp ground cinnamon

¼ tsp ground cloves

Mix all the ingredients well and store in a lidded container. You can also use a spice grinder to make it more like store-bought and to distribute the spices more evenly.

DIY Cajun Seasoning Blend

GLUTEN-FREE, SOY-FREE, NO OIL ADDED

This recipe will keep you in spicy goodness for a while and it's salt-free. It's a bonus that you can make it as spicy or mild as you want! This is used in the Cajun French Fry Po' Boy on page 95, the Southern Fried Okra on page 151 and the Mixed Veggie Hash on page 170.

MAKES ABOUT 2½ TBSP (20 G)

2 tsp (4 g) paprika

2 tsp (4 g) dried thyme

2 tsp (4 g) dried oregano or marjoram

I tsp (2 g) garlic powder

½ tsp onion powder

½–I tsp cayenne pepper (depending on heat preference)

¼ tsp black pepper

¼ tsp allspice

⅛ tsp cloves

Mix all the ingredients well and store in a lidded container. You can also use a spice grinder to make it more like store-bought and to distribute the spices more evenly.

Breakfast Seasoning Mix

GLUTEN-FREE, SOY-FREE, NO OIL ADDED

This turns plain tofu into a flavorful egg substitute. Try this in your tofu or chickpea scramble for an eggy taste.

MAKES ABOUT 3½ TSP (10 G)

½ tsp kala namak (or ¼ tsp regular salt)

½ tsp turmeric

½ tsp smoked paprika

½ tsp granulated garlic

½ tsp ground sage (or ¼ tsp rubbed sage)

¼ tsp ground black pepper

Mix the ingredients together and store in an airtight jar.

Healthy Snacks

Crispy Wonders from Your Air Fryer

I know that your desire for crispy and crunchy foods is what drew you to the air fryer in the first place. Here you'll find recipes for crunchy chickpeas that won't break the bank, all kinds of chips and even some cocoa almonds to satisfy your snacking sweet tooth.

Crunchy Cajun Chickpeas

GLUTEN-FREE, SOY-FREE, NO OIL ADDED OPTION*

Have you wanted to join the crispy chickpea snack craze? They are crazy expensive if you buy them premade. I have no idea why, since beans are very affordable dried or in cans.

Think of this recipe as a starting point and try your favorite seasoning blends like garam masala, chili powder or even cinnamon sugar.

If these chickpeas get soft, just reheat them in your air fryer to crisp them up!

MAKES ABOUT 1½ CUPS (170 G)

1 (15.5-oz [439-g]) can chickpeas, drained (or 1½ cups [225 g] homemade)

1 tsp (5 ml) olive oil (*or use aquafaba [page 22])

1½ tsp (4.5 g) DIY Cajun Seasoning Blend (page 65), or use store-bought

½ tsp salt (optional)

Mix the drained chickpeas in a bowl with the olive oil (or aquafaba), Cajun Seasoning Blend and salt, if using. Mix well to get all the chickpeas equally coated with the oil and spices.

Preheat your air fryer to 390°F (199°C) unless your model doesn't require it. Once it's hot, add the chickpeas to your air fryer basket.

Set the cooking time to 5 minutes, and when the time is up, shake or stir the chickpeas. Repeat for an additional 5 minutes.

If your chickpeas aren't as crisp as you'd like them to be at this point, shake again and cook for 3-minute intervals until they are. The time will vary depending on the size and model of your air fryer.

Let the chickpeas cool and store in an airtight container.

NOTE: Make sure to save the liquid from canned beans, called aquafaba, to use in other recipes. Store it in the fridge for up to 5 days.

SERVING SIZE: ½ cup (57 g), cooked • CALORIES: 88.7 • TOTAL FAT: 2.2 g • SODIUM: 235.8 mg • TOTAL CARBS: 13.5 g • DIETARY FIBER: 3.8 g • PROTEIN: 4.4 g

Cheesy Rosemary Roasted Edamame

GLUTEN-FREE, SOY-FREE OPTION*, NO OIL ADDED OPTION**

This is my favorite protein-packed snack. It's great to bring to the movies or have with your favorite beer or cocktail.

SERVES 8

1 (12-oz [340-g]) bag frozen shelled edamame (*substitute cooked chickpeas and cook a total of 10 minutes only)

2 tsp (10 ml) olive oil (**or use aquafaba [page 22])

1 tbsp (7 g) nutritional yeast

½ tsp salt

¼ tsp ground rosemary powder

⅛ tsp ground black pepper

Toss all the ingredients together in a mixing bowl, then add to your air fryer basket.

Cook at 390°F (200°C) for 5 minutes, then shake and cook 5 minutes more. Shake once more and cook for a final 5 minutes. You can cook an additional 5 minutes if they aren't crunchy. If you have leftovers, store in the fridge—but I bet you won't have any!

NOTE: You can make these into a quick lunch by only cooking for 10 minutes. They will still be soft but cooked through. Serve over steamed rice and enjoy!

AMOUNT PER SERVING: ¼ cup (about 38 g) · CALORIES: 81.1 · TOTAL FAT: 4.0 g · SODIUM: 148.4 mg · TOTAL CARBS: 6.3 g · DIETARY FIBER: 3.1 g · PROTEIN: 7.7 g

Cheesy Hot Sauce Collard Chips

GLUTEN-FREE, SOY-FREE, NO OIL ADDED OPTION*

Have you heard? Collard greens are the new kale! Did you know that a serving of collards has double the protein and iron that kale has? Collards even have more calcium. These chips will have you rethinking collards for sure.

MAKES ABOUT 1½ CUPS (ABOUT 55 G)

5 or 6 large collard leaves, stems removed and torn into bite-size pieces (about 4 cups [145 g] torn)

1 tsp (5 ml) mild oil or a few sprays of spray oil (*or use aquafaba [page 22])

1 tbsp (7 g) nutritional yeast

1 tsp (5 ml) hot sauce (use as mild or hot as you prefer)

¼ tsp salt (or less if your hot sauce is very salty)

Wash the collards well, then dry in a salad spinner or with a clean dish towel. Place in a large mixing bowl. Depending on what method you use, either spray with oil or drizzle the oil (or aquafaba) on the collards.

Massage the collards to spread the oil evenly, then sprinkle the nutritional yeast, hot sauce and salt on ½ teaspoon at a time and mix, repeating until everything is mixed well. Add the collards to your air fryer basket.

Set the temperature to 390°F (200°C) and cook 5 minutes, and when the time is up, shake or gently stir the collard chips. Cook an additional 2 to 3 minutes.

If your chips aren't as crisp as you'd like them to be at this point, shake again and cook for 30-second to 1-minute intervals until they are. Be very careful because they go from almost done to burned quickly. I would not recommend cooking for more than 1 minute at this point.

The time will vary depending on the size and model of your air fryer. Store in an airtight container.

NOTE: If you have a lid for your air fryer basket, now is a good time to try it out. If you don't have one, try putting a domed mesh strainer or steamer basket upside down to keep the light pieces from flying up into the heating element and burning.

NOTE: These are light and will fly up into the fan. An easy trick is to put a wire mesh rack on top. The ones that are made for air frying have about ½-inch (12-mm) legs to give the chips room to move. If you use this, you will need to remove it to shake the basket or the chips in the middle may stay soggy.

AMOUNT PER SERVING: 1½ cups (about 55 g) · CALORIES: 120.7 · TOTAL FAT: 5.0 g · SODIUM: 750.0 mg · TOTAL CARBS: 15.3 g · DIETARY FIBER: 8.1 g · PROTEIN: 7.2 g

Air Fryer Potato Chips

GLUTEN-FREE, SOY-FREE, NO OIL ADDED OPTION*

I know you are dying to make potato chips in your air fryer. They are fun to make! Don't wait until the last minute before you're having people over. You can make only about 2 servings in an average air fryer basket, so you'll need to cook a few batches to feed a crowd.

MAKES 2 SERVINGS

1 medium (168 g) potato (russet, red or yellow)

Spray oil as needed, up to 1 tbsp (15 ml) (*or use aquafaba [page 22])

Salt, to taste

Seasoning blend (optional)

NOTES: While I make many of the recipes in this book oil-free, I do find that these chips are more chiplike with the oil. Without the oil they seem more like dehydrated potatoes to me.

Be careful when using a mandoline—it is extremely sharp. Always use the hand guard that comes with it or buy a special cut-proof glove that you can use instead. I've learned the hard way, and I don't want you to!

Slice the potatoes using a mandoline. You can get an inexpensive handheld like the one I use instead of the larger, more expensive ones. You don't want to use the thinnest setting, but the second one, about 2.5 millimeters or the size of thick-cut kettle potato chips.

Place the potato slices in a large mixing bowl and cover with water. Let soak for 30 minutes to an hour.

Drain in a colander for another 30 minutes or dry using a clean dish towel or paper towel.

Put in a clean mixing bowl and spray with oil (or toss in aquafaba) to coat each chip and then salt to taste and mix again.

Add half to your air fryer and cook on 330°F (166°C) for 10 minutes, shake the basket and use tongs to separate any chips that are stuck on top of each other. Cook for another 10 minutes, shake and separate again. If the chips still aren't cooked enough, cook 3 to 5 minutes more or until the chips are 80 percent brown and not burned.

At any stage, you can remove chips that are done with tongs and keep cooking the rest.

There will still be a few places that look undercooked, but they will crisp up as they cool.

Repeat with the other half of the prepared potatoes.

AMOUNT PER SERVING: ½ of recipe • CALORIES: 52.5 • TOTAL FAT: 0.3 g • SODIUM: 0.0 mg • TOTAL CARBS: 13.0 g • DIETARY FIBER: 1.5 g • PROTEIN: 2.0 g

Dill Beet Chips

GLUTEN-FREE, SOY-FREE, NO OIL ADDED OPTION*

I love beets! There, I've said it and I hope you'll join me in proclaiming your feelings for the much-hated root veggie. These chips are delicate, crunchy bites that have a delicious dill flavor. Don't be afraid to experiment and try some of your other favorite seasoning blends on them too.

MAKES 1 SERVING

1 medium (82 g) beet, peeled and sliced thin with a mandoline

2 tsp (10 ml) olive oil (*or use aquafaba [page 22])

1½ tsp (3 g) Dill Seasoning Blend (page 54)

Salt to taste (optional)

Toss the beet slices in the olive oil (or aquafaba) and Dill Seasoning Blend. If you didn't add any salt to your dill seasoning, you may add some now if you'd like or leave them salt-free.

Place a single layer in your air fryer basket. Cook at 330°F (166°C) for 5 minutes. Separate pieces that are sticking together and give the basket a shake. I use tongs and crinkle up the individual slices.

Cook for 5 minutes more, repeat the separation of the beet slices and cook for a final 5 minutes.

If your beet slices are small in diameter, they may be done after the second 5 minutes; if large, they may need additional cooking time.

NOTE: They will crisp up more as they cool.

AMOUNT PER SERVING: 1 recipe • CALORIES: 114.8 • TOTAL FAT: 9.1 g • SODIUM: 64.0 mg • TOTAL CARBS: 7.8 g • DIETARY FIBER: 2.3 g • SUGARS: 5.5 g • PROTEIN: 1.3 g

Bow Tie Pasta Chips

GLUTEN-FREE OPTION*, SOY-FREE, NO OIL ADDED OPTION**

This is such a cute snack and a nice change of pace from pretzels and chips. The pasta crisps up and the flavors remind me a little of an Italian-style cheese cracker.

MAKES 4 SERVINGS

2 cups (152 g) dry whole wheat bow tie pasta (*use brown rice pasta)

1 tbsp (15 ml) olive oil (**or use aquafaba [page 22])

1 tbsp (7 g) nutritional yeast

1½ tsp (3 g) Italian Seasoning Blend (page 58)

½ tsp salt

Cook the pasta according to your package directions with the important exception of only cooking it for half the time listed, then drain the pasta well.

Toss the drained pasta with the olive oil (or aquafaba), nutritional yeast, Italian Seasoning Blend and salt.

Place about half of the mixture in your air fryer basket if yours is small; larger ones may be able to cook in one batch. Cook on 390°F (200°C) for 5 minutes. Shake the basket and cook 3 to 5 minutes more or until crunchy.

NOTE: These will crisp up more as they cool.

AMOUNT PER SERVING: ½ cup (about 40 g) • CALORIES: 141.5 • TOTAL FAT: 4.0 g • SODIUM: 291.1 mg • TOTAL CARBS: 21.7 g • DIETARY FIBER: 1.4 g • PROTEIN: 4.3 g

Becky Striepe's Bacon Cashews

GLUTEN-FREE, SOY-FREE, NO OIL ADDED

Becky's bacon cashews are ready when the pan is on the dry side and the cashews have darkened a bit. If you taste one while it's cooking, don't worry if it's a little bit chewy—like coconut bacon, these bacon cashews will get crunchier once they're cooled. See more of Becky's recipes on her site Glue and Glitter (glueandglitter.com).

MAKES ABOUT 3 CUPS (339 G)

3 cups (339 g) raw cashews
(I recommend whole cashews for this recipe, but you can use halves and pieces. Just reduce the baking time by a few minutes.)

2 tsp (4 g) salt

3 tbsp (45 ml) liquid smoke

2 tbsp (30 ml) blackstrap molasses

In a large bowl, toss together all the ingredients, making sure to coat the cashews really well (and really evenly!).

Pour the cashews into your air fryer basket and cook at 350°F (177°C) for 8 to 10 minutes, shaking every 2 minutes to make sure they cook evenly and to check for doneness.

NOTE: The variance in cooking time depends on a lot of things. Whole cashews will need more time; halves and pieces will need less (maybe even less than 8, so keep a close eye!). Humidity in your kitchen will also impact cooking time.

During the last 2 minutes, you should shake and check every minute to avoid burning. The line between done and burned can be thin with this recipe.

Let them cool to room temperature—about 10 to 15 minutes—then transfer to an airtight storage container and they should keep at least 3 days.

NOTE: Cashews can be expensive so I always buy halves and pieces because they are so much less. Check out Trader Joe's or your local Indian market to get some of the best prices.

AMOUNT PER SERVING: ¼ cup (28 g) • CALORIES: 187.8 • TOTAL FAT: 14.0 g • CHOLESTEROL: 0.0 mg • SODIUM: 396.9 mg • TOTAL CARBS: 10.0 g • DIETARY FIBER: 2.0 g • PROTEIN: 5.0 g

Cocoa Maple Almonds

GLUTEN-FREE, SOY-FREE, NO OIL ADDED

I love cocoa-coated almonds. My version has less sugar than the ones you can buy premade at the store, and they are less expensive too! For a variation, buy some vanilla powder and use it in place of the cocoa to make vanilla almonds.

MAKES 2 CUPS (240 G)

ALMOND INGREDIENTS

2 cups (240 g) raw almonds

1 tbsp (15 ml) maple syrup or agave (or liquid sweetener of your choice, to taste)

½ tsp vanilla extract

DRY COATING INGREDIENTS

1½ tbsp (8 g) cocoa powder (or raw cacao powder)

½ tsp salt (optional)

MAKE THE ALMONDS

Mix the almonds in a bowl with the maple syrup (or sweetener of your choice) and vanilla. Mix well to get all the almonds equally coated. Add the maple almonds to your air fryer basket.

Set the cooking time to 5 minutes and when the time is up, shake or stir the almonds. Repeat for an additional 3 to 5 minutes or until the nuts begin to get toasted.

Taste one of the almonds. If your almonds aren't as toasted as you'd like them to be at this point, shake again and cook for 3-minute intervals until they are. The time will vary depending on the size and model of your air fryer.

MAKE THE DRY COATING

Mix the cocoa powder and salt, if using, in a medium bowl. Add the hot almonds and toss well. The cocoa will stick to the warm coating. Let the almonds cool and store in an airtight container.

NOTES: Almonds will continue to cook as they cool, so you don't want to cook them very dark.

You can make this sugar-free by using stevia or monk fruit extract. You will use a few drops instead of the tablespoon of maple syrup that's called for, and up the vanilla from ½ to 1 teaspoon (5 ml) to help coat the almonds.

AMOUNT PER SERVING: ½ cup (60 g) • CALORIES: 179.3 • TOTAL FAT: 15.1 g • SODIUM: 145.7 mg • TOTAL CARBS: 8.3 g • DIETARY FIBER: 4.3 g • PROTEIN: 6.2 g

Cinnamon Apple Chips

GLUTEN-FREE, SOY-FREE, NO OIL ADDED

I always seem to have a few apples tucked away in the pantry and I love to experiment with new ways to use them. This is a quick and easy snack with all the flavors of fall. The maple syrup gives it an extra sugar crunch that's perfect!

MAKES 1 SERVING

1 small (125 g) apple, cored

2 tsp (10 ml) maple syrup or agave nectar

½ tsp ground cinnamon

Slice the apple into thin equal slices using the thinnest setting on your mandoline. Toss the apple slices with the maple syrup and cinnamon, then add a single layer to your air fryer basket (a little overlap is fine).

No matter what size air fryer you have, this will be cooked in 3 or 4 batches.

I like to place a mesh rack over these to help them not clump together.

Cook at 360°F (182°C) for 5 minutes, use a spoon or spatula and level out again, then cook 2 more minutes. They will crisp up more as they sit out to cool after about 2 minutes.

> **NOTE:** Some of my testers couldn't get the slices thin enough for them to crisp. If you can't, these still make wonderful sweet, healthy snacks. They will be more like baked apples instead of chips. How's that for a win-win?

AMOUNT PER SERVING: 1 recipe • CALORIES: 91.3 •
TOTAL FAT: 0.0 g • SODIUM: 2.1 mg • TOTAL CARBS: 24.8 g •
DIETARY FIBER: 3.6 g • PROTEIN: 0.0 g

Mains

Delightful Dinners That Will Have Your Family Asking for More

You are going to be amazed at how fast you can have dinner on the table using your air fryer. I've got some old favs like Country-Fried Cauliflower Steaks (page 110), tofu and soy curl stir-fries, even Vegan Mac and Cheese with a Surprise! (page 103). All the recipes can be made soy-free by substituting seitan or chickpeas, so they fit into most people's diets.

Cornmeal Battered Tofu

GLUTEN-FREE, SOY-FREE OPTION*, NO OIL ADDED OPTION**

This reminds me of a New Orleans–style fish fry. The lemon and wine marinade really elevates the tofu flavor, and the kelp will give it a bit of fishy flavor. Serve as is with homemade tartar sauce or as a po' boy sandwich.

MAKES 4 SERVINGS

1 (15- to 20-oz [425- to 567-g]) block super-firm or high-protein tofu (or firm tofu pressed overnight) *or 4 small cauliflower steaks

MARINADE INGREDIENTS

¼ cup (59 ml) white wine

¼ cup (59 ml) water

1 tbsp (7 g) nutritional yeast

2 tsp (5 ml) lemon juice

1 tsp (5 g) granulated kelp (optional)

1 tsp (5 g) sea salt (or salt of your choice)

½ tsp grated lemon peel (optional)

BATTER INGREDIENTS

¼ cup (28 g) cornmeal

¼ cup (59 ml) aquafaba

2 tbsp (30 ml) unsweetened nondairy milk

¼ tsp salt

½ cup (56 g) cornmeal

Spray oil (**or use aquafaba [page 22])

Cut the tofu into 8 thick "sticks." First cut in half to make 2 thinner slabs, then cut in half to make 4 smaller rectangles. Do the same with the cauliflower if you are using it.

MAKE THE MARINADE

Mix together the wine, water, nutritional yeast, lemon juice, kelp, if using, sea salt and lemon peel, if using. Add the tofu to the marinade for at least 1 hour.

MAKE THE BATTER

Mix the ¼ cup (28 g) of cornmeal, aquafaba, nondairy milk and salt in a small shallow pan. Add the ½ cup (56 g) of cornmeal to a second shallow pan.

Drag the tofu (or cauliflower) slices in the batter, let the extra batter drip off, then dredge in the cornmeal. Add to your air fryer basket. Repeat until the air fryer basket is full.

Spray the tops with oil if using. Cook on 370°F (188°C) for 15 minutes, then flip, spray more oil if using and cook 15 minutes more.

NOTE: Make a quick tartar sauce by mixing chopped dill pickles into vegan mayo with a sprinkling of ground celery seed.

AMOUNT PER SERVING: 2 sticks • CALORIES: 161.4 • TOTAL FAT: 5.4 g • SODIUM: 792.7 mg • TOTAL CARBS: 13.6 g • DIETARY FIBER: 2.3 g • PROTEIN: 18.9 g

Samosa Chaat

SOY-FREE

Most of you will know what a samosa is, but just in case you don't, it's a savory Indian pastry filled with potato, peas and spices. The word chaat takes it a step further into being a complete meal. You'll split the warm samosas in half, ladle some chickpea curry over them and then smother in tamarind and mint chutneys.

MAKES 6 SERVINGS (4 SAMOSAS EACH)

DOUGH INGREDIENTS

1½ cups (180 g) unbleached or whole wheat pastry flour

½ cup (120 ml) water

1 tsp (2 g) cumin seeds

½ tsp salt

3 tbsp (45 ml) olive oil

FILLING INGREDIENTS

1 tbsp (15 ml) oil

1 tsp (2 g) garam masala

½ tsp coriander seeds

½ tsp cumin seeds

¼ tsp ground cardamom

1 tsp (2 g) salt

⅛ tsp ground chile powder

3 cups (975 g) cooked cubed potatoes

1 cup (150 g) fresh or frozen green peas

CHICKPEA CURRY INGREDIENTS

1 tbsp (15 ml) oil

½ cup (75 g) minced onions

½ cup (118 ml) water

1 (15.5-oz [439-g]) can chickpeas, drained (or 1½ cups [439 g] homemade)

½ tsp minced ginger

½ tsp garlic

1 medium (123 g) tomato, minced

¾ tsp garam masala

½ tsp cumin seeds

⅛ tsp turmeric

⅛ tsp fenugreek seeds, optional

Pinch of chili powder

Salt, to taste

START THE DOUGH

In one bowl, mix the flour, water, cumin seeds, salt and olive oil until well combined. Let the dough sit 30 minutes while you make the samosa filling.

MAKE THE FILLING

Get the filling ready by heating the oil in a large sauté pan over medium heat. Once hot add the garam masala, coriander seeds, cumin seeds and ground cardamom, and sauté until fragrant, about 3 minutes.

Mix in the salt, ground chile powder, potatoes and green peas and cook until the peas are tender and ready to eat. You can add some water as needed if the pan cooks dry before it's ready.

(continued)

Samosa Chaat (Continued)

MAKE THE SAMOSAS

Separate the dough into 12 even pieces. Take one piece and use a rolling pin to make a circle that's about the thickness of a pie crust. Cut in half, pick one piece up and shape into a triangle. Roll the triangle up into a cone shape. Press the edges together while preserving the cone shape.

Take a few spoonfuls of the filling and press inside the cone firmly. Pull one side of the opening crust over and seal. Repeat until all the samosas are filled.

Cook the samosas on 350°F (177°C) for 15 minutes, check and cook 10 more minutes if the dough is still soft.

MAKE THE CURRY

While the samosas cook in the air fryer, make the chickpea curry. Heat the oil over medium heat in a saucepan and add the onions in once hot. Cook until the onions are translucent, then add the water, chickpeas, ginger, garlic, tomato, garam masala, cumin seeds, turmeric, fenugreek seeds, if using, chili powder and salt.

ASSEMBLE THE CHAAT

Cut the samosas in half, place in a bowl and ladle a scoop of chickpea curry over the samosas. You can top with mint chutney, tamarind sauce or plain vegan yogurt.

NOTE: Make these in no time by making them with spring roll wrappers. You will cook these in less time, so check every 5 minutes to see if they are getting brown and crispy.

AMOUNT PER SERVING: 4 samosas with ½ cup of curry (about 147 g) • **CALORIES:** 412.3 • **TOTAL FAT:** 14.1 g • **SODIUM:** 1043.6 mg • **DIETARY FIBER:** 11.2 g • **PROTEIN:** 9.9 g

Cajun French Fry Po' Boy with Vegan Mushroom Gravy

GLUTEN-FREE OPTION*, SOY-FREE OPTION**, NO OIL ADDED OPTION***

New Orleans is known for its delicious food, but did you know that it's also the home of the French Fry Po' Boy? Traditionally, French fries are sandwiched inside of a baguette and smothered with roast beef gravy. In this vegan version, we season and bake the fries to get a crispy crust. We also make a mushroom gravy that adds extra umami to your new favorite sandwich. You'll never miss the meat, and I promise you won't go hungry!

MAKES 4 SERVINGS

FRENCH FRY INGREDIENTS

4 medium Idaho russet potatoes, cut in half, then into planks

6 cups (1.4 L) boiling water, for soaking the potatoes

2 tsp (10 ml) olive oil (***or use aquafaba [page 22])

1 tsp (3 g) DIY Cajun Seasoning Blend (page 65)

½ tsp smoked paprika

½ tsp salt

¼ tsp granulated garlic

¼ tsp ground black pepper

MUSHROOM GRAVY INGREDIENTS

1 tbsp (15 ml) olive oil (***or use water)

3 cups (225 g) chopped mushrooms

2 tsp (10 ml) soy sauce (* and **or use coconut aminos)

2 tsp (10 ml) vegan Worcestershire sauce

½ cup (118 ml) water

1 tbsp (8 g) tapioca starch

SANDWICH OPTIONS

Fresh, soft loaf of French or Italian bread (or whole-grain or *gluten-free bread)

Sliced tomatoes

Lettuce

Vegan mayo

Tabasco or your favorite hot sauce

MAKE THE FRENCH FRIES

Place the cut fries in a heatproof bowl or saucepan. Bring the water to a boil and then pour it over the fries, covering them. I use my tea kettle, but you can even boil the water in a large saucepan and then add in the potatoes when you take it off the heat.

Let the potatoes soak in the hot water for 15 minutes, then pour into a strainer over the sink. Once mostly dry, toss the fries in the oil (or aquafaba), Cajun seasoning, paprika, salt, garlic and black pepper.

Add the potato mixture to your air fryer basket and cook at 350°F (177°C) for 5 minutes. Then shake the basket and cook 5 more minutes.

Raise the heat to 390°F (200°C) and cook for 5 minutes, then shake the basket and cook a final 5 minutes.

(continued)

Cajun French Fry Po' Boy with Vegan Mushroom Gravy (Continued)

MAKE THE MUSHROOM GRAVY

While the potatoes are cooking, heat 1 tablespoon (15 ml) of olive oil in a large skillet over medium heat. Once hot, add the mushrooms and sauté until they begin to release their juices. Stir in the soy sauce and Worcestershire sauce and cook for 2 more minutes.

Add the water and whisk in the tapioca starch. Turn the heat up to medium-high and cook until it thickens.

ASSEMBLE THE SANDWICHES

Slice the bread in half lengthwise. Toast the bread if you'd like or cut into smaller sandwich pieces. Slather vegan mayo and/or hot sauce on it or dress with lettuce, tomato and mayo.

Layer the baked fries over the bottom piece of the bread, and spread some of the mushroom mixture on top of the fries. Put on the top piece of bread and enjoy!

AMOUNT PER SERVING: 1 po' boy • CALORIES: 378.3 • TOTAL FAT: 6.7 g • SODIUM: 870.4 mg • TOTAL CARBS: 69.9 g • DIETARY FIBER: 7.3 g • PROTEIN: 12.0 g

Weeknight Calzones

SOY-FREE, NO OIL ADDED

While you can make pizza in your air fryer, to me it's even better when you make individual calzones instead. They cook so fast in the air fryer, and each person can customize one with his or her favorite fillings.

MAKES 2 CALZONES

¼ recipe Basic Whole Wheat Bread Dough (page 26)

½ cup (124 g) Extra-Tangy Cashew Cheese (page 37) or store-bought vegan mozzarella or ricotta

½ cup (55 g) chopped greens or spinach

Small amounts of any other fillings you want to add, like Roasted Garlic (page 38); roasted peppers; or chopped olives, tomatoes or summer squash

Tomato sauce, for serving

Divide the dough into 2 pieces and roll into thin ovals. You don't want the dough so thin that it tears. When I'm rolling the dough out I keep flipping it so it doesn't stick to the cutting board.

Spread the cheese on half the dough, then pile on your toppings. Repeat with the second calzone. Fold the dough over to make a half-moon shape, then crimp the dough around the edges to seal well.

Depending on the size of your air fryer, you may be able to cook only one at a time. Cook at 350°F (177°C) for 5 minutes, turn over and cook 5 minutes more. Repeat with the other calzone.

Serve sliced in half with a side of warm tomato sauce.

NOTES: If you want, use a perforated piece of parchment paper to make cleanup easier.

If you cook both at the same time, or your dough is extra thick, you may have to cook for a few minutes longer.

NOTES: Feel free to grab some premade pizza dough from the store if you don't have the time to bother with making your own dough. Or you can even make cheater pizzas using pita bread or English muffins.

Treat yourself to some of Miyoko's mozzarella to put in these when you can. I especially love her smoked mozzarella.

AMOUNT PER SERVING: 1 calzone • CALORIES: 441.9 • TOTAL FAT: 13.7 g • SODIUM: 902.1 mg • TOTAL CARBS: 63.0 g • DIETARY FIBER: 6.9 g • PROTEIN: 14.1 g

Teriyaki Soy Curl Dinner with Options

GLUTEN-FREE (IF NOT USING SEITAN), SOY-FREE OPTION*, NO OIL ADDED

This is a super easy last-minute dinner. I love the way soy curls get chewy when you air fry them, so they are my favorite in this. But it's delicious with tempeh or seitan too!

MAKES 4 SERVINGS

½ (8-oz [227-g]) bag soy curls (or 4 cups [474 g] tempeh or *seitan)

1 (16-oz [454-g]) bag frozen green beans, wax beans and baby carrots (known as Prince Edward mix) or frozen veggie mix of your choice

1 cup (240 ml) Easy Pineapple Teriyaki Sauce (page 49)

Cooked brown rice, for serving

Pour hot water to cover the soy curls in a heat-resistant bowl. This will reconstitute them. Then drain them in a strainer after about 10 to 15 minutes. (If you are using tempeh or seitan, skip this step.)

First, add the vegetables to your air fryer basket and cook on 350°F (177°C) for 10 minutes. They should be thawed but not roasted at this point.

Add the soy curls and cook for 10 minutes more.

Toss in the teriyaki sauce. Serve over steamed rice or cooked noodles.

> **NOTE:** Use a store-bought sauce if you don't have time to make homemade. Or make a double batch of sauce and freeze in 1 cup (240 ml) servings.

AMOUNT PER SERVING: ¼ of the recipe • CALORIES: 173.7 • TOTAL FAT: 4.6 g • CHOLESTEROL: 0.0 mg • SODIUM: 390.3 mg • TOTAL CARBS: 20.5 g • DIETARY FIBER: 6.0 g • PROTEIN: 11.7 g

Vegan Mac and Cheese with a Surprise!

GLUTEN-FREE OPTION*, SOY-FREE, NO OIL ADDED

There's no store-bought vegan cheese in this amazing casserole. Instead, it's full of homemade creamy vegan cheese sauce that actually uses a savory onion cream for its base. You can get the recipe on page 50. The flavor of the sauce mellows while it bakes and even my onion hater ate seconds!

MAKES 4 SERVINGS

SAUCE INGREDIENTS

1 cup (228 g) Savory Onion Cream (page 50), or substitute 1 cup (325 g) mashed cauliflower

3 tbsp (21 g) raw cashews, soaked overnight (or bring to a boil, remove from heat and let sit 15 minutes)

¼ cup (26 g) nutritional yeast

½ tsp granulated garlic powder

½ tsp smoked paprika

¼ tsp dry mustard powder

¼ tsp salt

⅛ tsp ground black pepper

2 cups (228 g) dry pasta, cooked according to the directions on the box (*use gluten-free)

¼ cup (28 g) panko breadcrumbs (*use gluten-free)

MAKE THE SAUCE

Place the Savory Onion Cream, cashews, nutritional yeast, garlic powder, smoked paprika, dry mustard powder, salt and black pepper into your blender and blend until smooth.

Pour the sauce on top of the cooked pasta and mix well. Get a nonstick pan that will fit in your size air fryer and either line with parchment paper or spray with a little oil. If you use parchment paper, cut the edges of the paper so it doesn't go over the top of the pan because it could burn on the heat element.

Add in the pasta mixture and top with the panko. Cover the pan with aluminum foil (or an oven-safe lid) and cook for 15 minutes on 350°F (177°C). Remove foil and cook 5 to 10 minutes more, until the panko is browned.

NOTES: If you really hate onions in any form you can still make this. Just substitute 1 cup (325 g) of mashed cauliflower or potato for the Savory Onion Cream.

If you want this creamier, you can always double the sauce, or just double the cashews in it.

AMOUNT PER SERVING: ½ cup (50 g) pasta and ¼ cup (63 g) of sauce · CALORIES: 307.4 · TOTAL FAT: 4.1 g · SODIUM: 449.4 mg · TOTAL CARBS: 55.4 g · DIETARY FIBER: 5.2 g · PROTEIN: 12.0 g

Air-Fried Seitan and Veggies with Peanut Sauce

GLUTEN-FREE OPTION*, SOY-FREE OPTION**, NO OIL ADDED

This is an easy last-minute dinner that you can make no matter how tired you are. You can even make the sauce ahead of time! If you'd like to spice up the sauce, feel free to add some cayenne powder or sriracha sauce.

MAKES 4 SERVINGS

4 cups (16 oz [453 g]) frozen broccoli, carrots and/or cauliflower

2 cups (400 g) seitan, cut in chunks (*or use chickpeas or tofu) store-bought or see recipe on page 42

¾ cup (180 ml) water

½ cup (128 g) peanut butter

1 tbsp (15 ml) plus 2 tsp (10 ml) soy sauce (* and ** use coconut aminos)

2 tsp (10 ml) rice wine vinegar

¾ tsp ground ginger

¼ tsp granulated garlic

Sriracha, to taste (optional)

Add the vegetables to your air fryer basket and cook for 350°F (177°C) for 10 minutes.

Shake the basket, add the seitan and cook 10 minutes more, or until the veggies are tender and the seitan begins to get a little crispy.

While the veggies and seitan are cooking, make the sauce by combining the water, peanut butter, soy sauce, vinegar, ginger, garlic and sriracha, if using, in a small mixing bowl. Whisk until smooth.

Serve the air fryer mixture over cooked rice, raw spinach or on its own. Just make sure it's smothered in peanut sauce because that's what makes this recipe amazing.

AMOUNT PER SERVING: 1½ cups (175 g) • CALORIES: 373.2 • TOTAL FAT: 17.6 g • SODIUM: 910.5 mg • TOTAL CARBS: 41.0 g • DIETARY FIBER: 8.3 g • PROTEIN: 14.9 g

Cherry Bourbon BBQ Tofu or Cauliflower

GLUTEN-FREE, SOY-FREE OPTION*, NO OIL ADDED OPTION**

You will feel so empowered after you make your first batch of BBQ sauce. For the Cherry Bourbon BBQ Sauce, you just need to toss everything in a blender and it's ready to use! It turns plain tofu or cauliflower into a meal that will quickly become your favorite.

MAKES 4 SERVINGS

1 (15- to 20-oz [425- to 567-g]) block super-firm or high-protein tofu, cut into cubes (or firm tofu pressed overnight or *4 cups [500 g] cauliflower florets)

A few spritzes of oil (**or use aquafaba [page 22])

2 tbsp (16 g) finely ground cornmeal

½ cup (120 ml) Cherry Bourbon BBQ Sauce (page 108)

Add the tofu or cauliflower to a bowl and spritz with oil (or aquafaba). Sprinkle the cornmeal over the mixture and toss to lightly coat.

Preheat your air fryer to 390°F (199°C) unless your model doesn't require it. Once it's hot, add the coated tofu to your air fryer basket.

Set the cooking time to 5 minutes, and when the time is up shake or stir the tofu. Repeat for an additional 5 minutes.

Toss the cooked tofu or cauliflower in the Cherry Bourbon BBQ Sauce (page 108). Serve with roasted corn or your favorite sides.

> **NOTES:** If you'd like to make cleanup easier, you can use a piece of perforated parchment paper in the basket, under the tofu.
>
> If you are using cauliflower, you may need to cook for another 5 minutes to get the cauliflower tender.

AMOUNT PER SERVING: 1 cup • CALORIES: 179.0 • TOTAL FAT: 5.1 g • CHOLESTEROL: 0.0 mg • SODIUM: 237.0 mg • TOTAL CARBS: 18.7 g • DIETARY FIBER: 1.8 g • PROTEIN: 18.0 g

Cherry Bourbon BBQ Sauce

GLUTEN-FREE, SOY-FREE, NO OIL ADDED

This thick and rich BBQ sauce is sweet from the cherries and a little bit tart from the apple cider vinegar. All the other ingredients blend in to make my favorite BBQ sauce of all time.

MAKES ABOUT 1 CUP (ABOUT 256 G)

½ cup (56 g) pitted cherries (thawed if frozen)

¼ cup (60 ml) maple syrup

2 tbsp (30 ml) apple cider vinegar

2 tbsp (32 g) tomato paste

1 tbsp (15 ml) bourbon or whiskey (use apple juice if you don't use alcohol)

1 tbsp (15 ml) molasses

¾ tsp granulated garlic

½ tsp onion powder

½ tsp liquid smoke

½ tsp salt (or to taste)

¼ tsp ground black pepper

¼ tsp ancho chili powder (or to taste and you can use chipotle to make it spicier as well)

Add all of the ingredients to your blender and blend until smooth. You may have to scrape down the sides of the blender a few times.

Store in the fridge or freeze leftovers in ice cube trays.

SERVINGS PER RECIPE: 4 · AMOUNT PER SERVING: ¼ cup (64 g) · CALORIES: 94.1 · TOTAL FAT: 0.1 g · SODIUM: 360.1 mg · TOTAL CARBS: 22.0 g · DIETARY FIBER: 0.8 g · PROTEIN: 0.6 g

Stove-Top Black Pepper White Gravy

NO OIL ADDED

This is my go-to gravy and I put it on anything country fried. It's also amazing with some vegan sausage crumbled up in it over freshly baked biscuits.

MAKES ABOUT 1 CUP (120 ML)

2 tbsp (14 g) white whole wheat flour (or brown rice flour)

1 cup (120 ml) soy milk (or any nondairy milk)

½ tsp salt

⅛–¼ tsp black pepper, or to taste

Toast the flour over low heat in a small, dry skillet until fragrant and light brown, about 3 minutes. Be sure to stir a few times a minute so the flour doesn't burn.

Whisk in the soy milk (or nondairy milk), salt and pepper. Turn up the heat to medium high. Whisk until it begins to come to a boil.

The moment it turns from thin to medium thick, remove from the stove-top and keep whisking. If it's a little thin, cook longer, and if it gets too thick, thin it with more nondairy milk.

AMOUNT PER SERVING: ¼ cup (30 ml) · CALORIES: 35.3 · TOTAL FAT: 0.9 g · SODIUM: 315.7 mg · TOTAL CARBS: 4.3 g · DIETARY FIBER: 0.7 g · PROTEIN: 2.0 g

---

Country-Fried Cauliflower Steaks

GLUTEN-FREE OPTION*, SOY-FREE, NO OIL ADDED

Eating healthy does not mean missing out on family favorites. This plant-based recipe gets a bite from the thick cauliflower stems that hold these steaks together. The two-step coating is the secret to its crispy goodness. Smother it in some oil-free gravy and you have a decadent dinner you can have any time!

MAKES 4 SERVINGS

2 (½-in [12-mm] thick) middle cuts from a whole head of cauliflower, cut in half to make 4 pieces

½ cup (56 g) white whole wheat flour (*or brown rice flour)

¾ cup (180 ml) soy milk (or any nondairy milk)

½ tsp apple cider vinegar

¾ tsp marjoram

¾ tsp thyme

¼ tsp salt

⅛ tsp pepper

½ cup (56 g) whole wheat panko breadcrumbs (*use gluten-free)

Cook cauliflower steaks (unbreaded at this point) in your air fryer for 10 minutes at 350°F (177°C).

Make 2 dipping stations in pans that your cauliflower pieces will fit in. In the first, add the flour, soy milk (or nondairy milk), apple cider vinegar, marjoram, thyme, salt and pepper. Spread the breadcrumbs in the second one.

Dip the cauliflower steak into the batter (use tongs if they are still hot). Flip with tongs to coat the other side with batter. Then carefully place into the breadcrumbs. Spoon breadcrumbs on any bald spaces, then flip. Press the breadcrumbs with your hand so that they adhere to the batter, and carefully place in your air fryer basket. Repeat until all the steaks are coated.

Cook for 330°F (166°C) for 5 minutes, then flip and cook 5 minutes more. Serve topped with Stove-Top Black Pepper White Gravy (page 109) or steamed rice or mashed potatoes.

AMOUNT PER SERVING: 1 cauliflower steak • CALORIES: 137.8 • TOTAL FAT: 1.5 g • SODIUM: 73.4 mg • TOTAL CARBS: 25.0 g • DIETARY FIBER: 6.3 g • PROTEIN: 7.5 g

Potato Kofta with an Easy Creamy Curry Sauce (Aloo Kofta)

GLUTEN-FREE, SOY-FREE, NO OIL ADDED OPTION*

This is my easy version of one of my favorite creamy Indian curries. It's very mild, so it's a great way to introduce your family to a new cuisine. The potato fritters, or koftas, are cooked in your air fryer. I like to serve mine with steamed brown basmati rice and smothered in the easy curry sauce.

MAKES 16 KOFTAS WITH ABOUT 2½ CUPS (600 ML) CURRY SAUCE

KOFTA INGREDIENTS

2 cups (650 g) mashed potatoes

1 tsp (5 g) minced ginger

½ tsp minced garlic

½ tsp salt

½ tsp ground turmeric

¼ tsp ground cumin

⅛ tsp ground cardamom

2 tbsp (16 g) chickpea flour

Mild spray oil for cooking (optional)

CURRY SAUCE INGREDIENTS

1 tbsp (15 ml) oil (*or water sauté)

½ cup (75 g) minced onion

½ tsp minced garlic

½ tsp garam masala

¼ tsp ground cumin

¼ tsp ground turmeric

⅛ tsp ground cardamom

1 tsp grated ginger

2 cups (400 g) chopped tomatoes

½ cup (120 ml) water

¼ cup (40 g) raw cashews

½ tsp salt

MAKE THE KOFTAS

Add the cooked mashed potatoes, ginger, garlic, salt, turmeric, cumin and cardamom to a medium mixing bowl and mix well. Form the mixture into tablespoon-size (13-g) balls and roll in the flour. Repeat until all the koftas are formed. You can spray with oil if using.

Cook in your air fryer at 390°F (200°C) for 10 minutes or until the outside begins to crisp up.

MAKE THE SAUCE

Heat the oil over medium heat in a large sauté pan with a lid. Once the oil is hot, add the onion and cook until translucent over medium heat. Stir in the garlic, garam masala, cumin, turmeric and cardamom.

Cook until the spices become fragrant, then add the ginger, tomatoes, water and cashews and cover. Simmer over low heat for 10 minutes or until the tomatoes and cashews soften.

Carefully transfer the hot mixture to your blender. Add the salt and blend until silky smooth.

Ladle the warm sauce over the warm koftas and enjoy with steamed basmati rice, roti or your favorite Indian bread.

AMOUNT PER SERVING: 4 koftas and ½ cup (120 ml) sauce • CALORIES: 272.3 • TOTAL FAT: 7.8 g • SODIUM: 878.5 mg • TOTAL CARBS: 49.8 g • DIETARY FIBER: 6.0 g • PROTEIN: 8.8 g

Whole Foods Arancini di Riso (Italian Rice Balls)

GLUTEN-FREE OPTION*, SOY-FREE, NO OIL ADDED

Just so you know, these are my whole foods variation of a traditional dish. We'll use brown rice in place of white Arborio and add flavor with nutritional yeast and spices. If you want, you can put a surprise in the middle, like vegan cheese, a pitted olive or another savory treasure.

MAKES 8 (ABOUT ½ CUP EACH OR ABOUT 100 G) ARANCINI

4 cups (680 g) cooked brown rice

¼ cup (27 g) nutritional yeast

¼–½ cup (59–118 ml) unsweetened nondairy milk, as needed

2 tbsp (13 g) ground flax seed mixed with 4 tbsp (60 ml) warm water

1 tsp (2 g) dried basil

½ tsp dried oregano

½ tsp salt

¼ tsp black pepper

⅛ tsp powdered rosemary

¼–½ cup (28–56 g) whole wheat breadcrumbs (*or use gluten-free breadcrumbs)

Add the cooked brown rice, nutritional yeast, ¼ cup (60 ml) of the nondairy milk, ground flax mixture, basil, oregano, salt, pepper and rosemary to a large mixing bowl and combine well.

Form ½ cup (120 ml) of the rice mixture into a ball. If the mixture is too dry, add extra nondairy milk 1 tablespoon (15 ml) at a time until it's wet enough to hold its shape.

Then roll in the breadcrumbs and set in the air fryer basket. Depending on the size of your air fryer, you may need to do this in multiple batches.

Cook at 350°F (177°C) for 10 to 15 minutes, or until hot in the middle and crunchy on the outside.

AMOUNT PER SERVING: ½ cup (100 g) ball • CALORIES: 162.0 • TOTAL FAT: 2.1 g • SODIUM: 158.5 mg • TOTAL CARBS: 31.1 g • DIETARY FIBER: 4.0 g • PROTEIN: 5.0 g

Air-Fried Pupusas

GLUTEN-FREE, SOY-FREE OPTION*, NO OIL ADDED OPTION**

Pupusas are fun to create, so be sure to include your family and friends when you make them. To make the pupusas, you flatten a ball of masa dough, add a small amount of filling in the middle, then carefully gather the dough into a ball around the filling. Then you can press it down flat again and air fry it. It's great to use up the last bit of your refried beans!

MAKES 6 PUPUSAS

1¼ cups (142 g) masa (ground corn flour treated with lime)

1–1¼ cups (240–300 ml) water

¼ tsp salt

½ cup (120 ml) filling of your choice (soy chorizo, *refried beans, vegan cheese, chopped BBQ riblets, etc.)

Spray oil, for cooking (**optional)

Make the dough by adding the masa, 1 cup (240 ml) of the water and salt to a mixing bowl. Stir until combined.

Grab a golf ball–size ball of dough and smash it flat in the palm of your hand. If you see lots of cracking, then you need to add more water to the dough and try again. Mix in another ¼ cup (60 ml) of water and test again. Repeat until dough stays together when pressed but does not stick to your hand.

To make the pupusas, divide the dough into 6 golf ball–size balls and set on a cutting board. The balls will be about 2 tablespoons (30 ml) each.

Take a ball and smash it down, keeping it thicker than a regular pie crust would be. Put a heaping teaspoon of filling in the middle and gently bring the edges together, forming another ball with the filling in the center.

Roll the ball in your hand and try to form the dough in even thickness surrounding the filling. If you have a thin spot it will break or crack in the next step.

Lightly smash the ball into a patty, then repeat until all 6 pupusas are ready.

Place 2 or more in your air fryer basket, depending on its size. Spritz with oil, if using, and cook at 330°F (166°C) for 5 minutes. Flip, spritz with oil on the other side if you're using it and cook 5 minutes more.

NOTES: You can use a piece of perforated parchment paper under the pupusas.

Try the Roasted Tomatillo Green Salsa from page 33 on these. I think they are great together.

AMOUNT PER SERVING: 1 pupusa · CALORIES: 88.6 · TOTAL FAT: 2.8 g · SATURATED FAT: 0.4 g · POLYUNSATURATED FAT: 0.3 g · MONOUNSATURATED FAT: 0.2 g · CHOLESTEROL: 0.0 mg · SODIUM: 246.9 mg · POTASSIUM: 47.9 mg · TOTAL CARBS: 14.0 g · DIETARY FIBER: 2.4 g · SUGARS: 0.4 g · PROTEIN: 3.4 g

Easy Air Fry Seitan Riblets

SOY-FREE, NO OIL ADDED

This may be the easiest seitan you ever make. It goes through two baking cycles. After the first, it's still a bit wet and easy to cut into strips. The second cook makes them nice and chewy.

MAKES 4 SERVINGS

1 cup (120 g) vital wheat gluten

¼ cup (27 g) nutritional yeast

1 tsp (2 g) mushroom powder or vegan Worcestershire sauce

1 tsp (2 g) onion powder

1 tsp (2 g) salt (optional)

½ tsp garlic powder

¾ cup (177 ml) water or unsalted vegetable broth

¼ cup (60 ml) BBQ sauce

Add the vital wheat gluten, nutritional yeast, mushroom powder (or vegan Worcestershire sauce), onion powder, salt and garlic powder to your food processor.

Pulse until mixed well. Let the flour settle, then drizzle the water in through the top opening while you have the processor on.

Then let the food processor run for about 3 minutes more to knead the seitan. Remove the dough and put it on a cutting board and knead a little bit more with your hands.

Press and pull the dough into a circle that will fit into your air fryer basket. Then cut it in half so that it will cook a little faster and more evenly.

Place the 2 seitan pieces into your air fryer and cook on 370°F (188°C) for 8 minutes. Then flip the pieces over and cook 5 minutes more.

You could stop here and cut into chunks to use in stir-fries, slice thin for sandwiches or cut into pieces and pulse in your food processor to make ground seitan for tacos or spaghetti sauce.

Or go ahead and make riblets! Slice half of the seitan into ½-inch (12-mm) wide strips, then toss with about ¼ cup (60 ml) of your favorite BBQ sauce. Place in an oven-safe container that fits into your air fryer and cook at 370°F (188°C) for 5 minutes.

AMOUNT PER SERVING: ¼ of recipe or about 1 cup • CALORIES: 142.8 • TOTAL FAT: 0.9 g • SATURATED FAT: 0.1 g • POLYUNSATURATED FAT: 0.2 g • MONOUNSATURATED FAT: 0.0 g • CHOLESTEROL: 0.0 mg • SODIUM: 624.7 mg • POTASSIUM: 171.3 mg • TOTAL CARBS: 9.5 g • DIETARY FIBER: 1.9 g • SUGARS: 0.5 g • PROTEIN: 25.8 g

Teff Veggie Burgers

GLUTEN-FREE, SOY-FREE, NO OIL ADDED OPTION*

Teff, a whole grain, has protein and fiber and is the perfect choice to include in your homemade veggie burgers. These are made of cooked teff mixed with kidney beans and sautéed vegetables. You can substitute a different bean like pintos or black beans, and you can add spice blends like chili powder or garam masala if you want your burger to have an international flair.

MAKES 8 PATTIES

TEFF INGREDIENTS

2 cups (473 ml) water

⅔ cup (168 g) brown teff grain

SAUTÉ INGREDIENTS

1 tbsp (15 ml) olive oil (*or use water sauté)

1 cup (142 g) minced onion

1 cup (78 g) minced mushrooms

1 medium carrot (61 g), grated

2 cloves (6 g) minced garlic

1½ tsp (3 g) salt

¼ tsp black pepper

BURGER INGREDIENTS

1 (15.5-oz [439-g]) can kidney beans, drained and rinsed (or 1½ cups [439 g] homemade)

¼ cup (27 g) nutritional yeast

NOTE: You can freeze leftovers for another dinner, crumble into pasta sauces or make a taco filling.

MAKE THE TEFF

Bring the 2 cups (473 ml) of water to boil in a saucepan with a cover. Once it boils, stir in the teff, reduce to a simmer, cover and cook 15 to 20 minutes until the teff is cooked.

MAKE THE SAUTÉ

Heat the oil (*or water) in a large sauté pan over medium heat. Once hot, add the onion and sauté until translucent. Stir in the mushrooms, carrots, garlic, salt and pepper. Cook until the mushrooms have released all their liquid, the carrots are tender and the sauté mixture is dry.

MAKE THE BURGERS

Add the drained kidney beans to a mixing bowl and mash with a potato masher until all of the beans are broken up. Add in the cooked teff. It will be clumped up, but mash it in with the potato masher just like you did for the beans. Mix in the sautéed veggies and nutritional yeast. Divide the mixture into 8 balls. Flatten the balls into patties and place 2 to 4 in your air fryer, depending on its size.

Set your air fryer to 330°F (166°C). Cook 10 minutes on one side, until they are solid enough to easily flip. Then flip and cook on the other side until they are no longer mushy in the middle, about 10 minutes more.

AMOUNT PER SERVING: 1 patty • CALORIES: 136.3 • TOTAL FAT: 2.4 g • SATURATED FAT: 0.3 g • SODIUM: 610.2 mg • POTASSIUM: 272.2 mg • TOTAL CARBS: 23.8 g • DIETARY FIBER: 6.6 g • SUGARS: 0.5 g • PROTEIN: 6.7 g

Crispy Coconut Tofu Nuggets

GLUTEN-FREE OPTION*, NO OIL ADDED

This is my new favorite way to serve tofu. It has a burst of coconut flavor and lots of crunch. I serve mine with a sweet Thai chili sauce, but they are great on their own too.

MAKES 4 SERVINGS

BATTER INGREDIENTS

½ cup (56 g) white whole wheat flour (*or brown rice flour)

1 cup (240 ml) canned coconut milk

2 tsp (20 ml) soy sauce (*use gluten-free soy sauce or coconut aminos)

DRY COATING INGREDIENTS

1 cup (80 g) finely shredded coconut

¾ cup (47 g) panko breadcrumbs

1 (14-oz [397-g]) package extra-firm or super-firm tofu (or firm tofu, pressed), cut into cubes

FOR SERVING

Sweet Thai chili garlic sauce for dipping

MAKE THE BATTER

Mix the flour, coconut milk and soy sauce in a bowl.

MAKE THE DRY COATING

Next, mix the coconut and panko in a second shallow dish.

Dip the tofu cubes in the wet batter, then put into the dry. You will need to press the dry on with your hand firmly. Then place on the bottom of your air fryer basket. Repeat until all the tofu is coated.

Preheat your air fryer to 390°F (199°C) unless your model doesn't require it. Once it's hot, carefully add the coconut tofu to your air fryer basket.

Set the cooking time to 5 minutes, and when the time is up, check to see how brown it is. Depending on your air fryer size, you will cook for an additional 3 to 5 minutes.

Repeat until all the tofu is cooked. How many times that takes will depend on the size of your air fryer. Serve with the chili garlic sauce.

AMOUNT PER SERVING: 1 cup (about 100 g) • CALORIES: 342.9 • TOTAL FAT: 23.3 g • SATURATED FAT: 16.5 g • POLYUNSATURATED FAT: 0.0 g • MONOUNSATURATED FAT: 0.0 g • CHOLESTEROL: 0.0 mg • SODIUM: 146.2 mg • POTASSIUM: 2.9 mg • TOTAL CARBOHYDRATE: 22.6 g • DIETARY FIBER: 4.5 g • SUGARS: 2.4 g • PROTEIN: 14.2 g

---

Summer by the Beach Vegetable Patties

GLUTEN-FREE OPTION*, SOY-FREE, NO OIL ADDED

These crispy little patties are the perfect summer dinner and are even better when slathered with homemade Vegan Tartar Sauce (page 126).

MAKES 8 PATTIES

1 (15.5-oz [439-g]) can white beans (cannellini, navy, etc.), liquid reserved for aquafaba

1 cup (170 g) shredded zucchini

1 cup (99 g) shredded carrots

1 cup (142 g) corn kernels

1 tsp (2 g) celery seeds

¾ tsp salt, or to taste

½ tsp tarragon

½ tsp cayenne powder

½ tsp paprika

¼ tsp ground black pepper

⅛ tsp dry mustard powder

⅛ tsp ground allspice

½ cup (60 g) panko breadcrumbs (*use gluten-free)

Mash the beans in a large mixing bowl. Place the zucchini and carrot into a strainer and press the liquid out. You just need to get most of it, so don't worry if you don't get every drop.

Mix the zucchini, carrots, corn kernels, celery seeds, salt, tarragon, cayenne, paprika, black pepper, mustard powder and allspice into the mashed beans.

Add the breadcrumbs to a flat dish. Make patties with ¼ cup (60 ml) of the mixture and then place into the breadcrumbs. Pat the breadcrumbs onto the patties so they will stay on.

Place however many patties fit into your air fryer basket. Cook on 350°F (177°C) for 10 minutes, then carefully flip and cook 5 minutes more.

Repeat until all the patties are cooked. Serve as is, topped with tartar sauce (page 126) or on a sandwich.

NOTE: If you'd like to make cleanup easier, you can use a piece of perforated parchment paper in the basket, under the patties.

SERVING SIZE: 1 patty • AMOUNT PER SERVING: 1 patty • CALORIES: 91.1 • TOTAL FAT: 0.2 g • SODIUM: 498.0 mg • TOTAL CARBS: 19.4 g • DIETARY FIBER: 4.3 g • PROTEIN: 4.6 g

Vegan Tartar Sauce

GLUTEN-FREE, SOY-FREE OPTION*, NO OIL ADDED

This is a quick and easy way to whip up the perfect sauce for your tofu sticks. It has no oil added like the mayo version, and you can make it with soy-free vegan yogurt if you are allergic to soy.

MAKES JUST UNDER 1 CUP (245 G)

½ cup (112 g) unsweetened plain vegan yogurt (*use coconut or almond)

¼ cup (61 g) dill pickle relish

2 tbsp (30 ml) lemon juice

1 tsp (1 g) fresh tarragon (or ½ tsp dried)

Mix all the ingredients together. Store any leftovers in the fridge for up to 3 days.

AMOUNT PER SERVING: ¼ cup (61 g) • CALORIES: 15.6 • TOTAL FAT: 0.9 g • SODIUM: 237.3 mg • TOTAL CARBS: 1.8 g • DIETARY FIBER: 0.8 g • PROTEIN: 0.2 g

Kathy's Super Easy Stir-Fry Sauce

GLUTEN-FREE, NO OIL ADDED OPTION*

This is my easy-peasy stir-fry sauce. It takes no time to whip up, so you can make it any day of the week.

MAKES 4 SERVINGS

½ cup (120 ml) water

¼ cup (60 ml) orange juice

¼ cup (60 ml) gluten-free soy sauce (Bragg's aminos or coconut aminos)

3 tbsp (45 ml) maple syrup or agave nectar (or sweetener of your choice, to taste)

2 tsp (6 g) chopped ginger

1 tsp (5 ml) sesame oil (*use tahini)

1 tsp (3 g) minced garlic

Add all the ingredients to a mason jar or a salad dressing shaker. Put the top on well and shake. You'll need to shake again right before using.

AMOUNT PER SERVING: ¼ cup (60 ml) • CALORIES: 66.2 • TOTAL FAT: 1.2 g • SODIUM: 900.7 mg • TOTAL CARBS: 13.2 g • DIETARY FIBER: 0.2 g • PROTEIN: 1.2 g

Crispy Tofu with Broccoli and Carrots Stir-Fry

GLUTEN-FREE, NO OIL ADDED OPTION*

Your air fryer has the ability to make plain, rubbery tofu into something so amazing that tofu haters will be asking for more. You could just make the air-fried tofu and eat with a dip, but this recipe uses it in a stir-fry that you make on your stove while the tofu is cooking. Serve it over cooked noodles, steamed brown rice or quinoa to complete the meal.

MAKES 4 SERVINGS

TOFU INGREDIENTS

1 (14-oz [397-g]) package extra-firm tofu, pressed and cut into cubes

1 tbsp (15 ml) sesame oil (*or use aquafaba [page 22])

1 tbsp (15 ml) low-sodium soy sauce

3 tbsp (24 g) organic cornstarch (or tapioca starch)

STIR-FRY INGREDIENTS

1 recipe Kathy's Super Easy Stir-Fry Sauce (page 127), or your favorite stir-fry sauce

2 cups (256 g) carrot coins

4 cups (700 g) broccoli (fresh or frozen)

1 tsp (3 g) cornstarch (or tapioca starch)

FOR SERVING

2 cups (316 g) cooked brown rice or quinoa

MAKE THE TOFU

Toss the pressed tofu with the sesame oil (or aquafaba) and soy sauce to mix well. Sprinkle half the cornstarch over the tofu and toss. Repeat and make sure the tofu is coated evenly.

Preheat your air fryer to 390°F (199°C) unless your model doesn't require it. Once it's hot, add the coated tofu to your air fryer basket. Set the cooking time to 5 minutes, and when the time is up, shake or stir the tofu. Repeat for an additional 5 minutes.

MAKE THE STIR-FRY

While the tofu is air frying, heat all but 1 tablespoon (15 ml) of the stir-fry sauce in a large sauté pan or wok over medium heat. Add the carrots and cook until almost tender, then add the broccoli and sauté until they are tender and still bright green.

Add the additional cornstarch to the reserved sauce and mix in with a fork until smooth. Add this last bit of sauce with the cooked tofu and mix well. Once the sauce has thickened remove from heat and serve over rice or quinoa.

AMOUNT PER SERVING: 1½ cups (about 150 g) • CALORIES:195 • TOTAL FAT: 6.8 g • SODIUM: 1,129.0 mg • TOTAL CARBS: 26.6 g • DIETARY FIBER: 5.0 g • PROTEIN: 10.5 g

Black Bean Avocado Chimichangas

GLUTEN-FREE OPTION*, SOY FREE, NO OIL ADDED

Air fryers magically turn plain burritos into crispy chimichangas. The best part is that you need no oil to do it. While I add specific ingredients in this recipe, you can add in your favorite burrito ingredients and use the same cooking time.

MAKES 4 SERVINGS

4 Ezekiel sprouted whole-grain tortillas or other whole-grain burrito-size tortillas (*use gluten-free tortilla)

1 cup (238 g) refried black beans (or plain black beans mixed with a few tablespoons of your favorite salsa)

1 large (136 g) or 2 small ripe avocados, sliced

OPTIONAL FILLINGS

½ cup (56 g) shredded vegan cheese

1 tbsp (14 g) green chiles

½ cup (114 g) Savory Onion Cream (page 50)

OPTIONAL TOPPINGS

Shredded lettuce

Chopped fresh tomatoes

Chopped cilantro

Vegan sour cream

Salsa

Roasted Tomatillo Green Salsa (page 33)

Savory Onion Cream (page 50)

Soften the tortillas by placing them in the microwave for 20 seconds or by steaming over a pan of boiling water for a few seconds. If your tortillas are already pliable, you can skip this step.

Spread ¼ cup (64 g) of the beans lengthwise in the middle of the tortilla, and place slices of avocado and any of the optional fillings you want to use on top of that. Fold the ends in and roll up into a burrito.

Place seam-side down in your air fryer basket. You should be able to fit at least 2 in at a time. In a larger air fryer, you may be able to fit all 4.

Cook at 330°F (166°C) for 10 minutes, then cook at 400°F (205°C) for 5 minutes or until browned and crispy. Serve with all the toppings you want to pile on top.

AMOUNT PER SERVING: 1 chimichanga • CALORIES: 285.0 • TOTAL FAT: 11.0 g • SODIUM: 362.5 mg • TOTAL CARBS: 37.0 g • DIETARY FIBER: 10.5 g • PROTEIN: 10.0 g

---

Side Dishes and Appetizers
Fried Favorites Lightened Up with Air Frying

These side dishes will make any sandwich into a magically satisfying meal. Homemade tots, hush puppies, corn on the cob, air-fried "baked" potatoes and so much more. You can even try the Sesame, Ginger and Garlic Edamame (page 155) or the Stuffed Artichoke with Fresh Herbs (page 156) as a light summer meal!

Plain Old Tots

GLUTEN-FREE, SOY-FREE, NO OIL ADDED OPTION*

Tater tots are a strange thing. Invented by Ore-Ida in the 1950s to use up the leftover slivers of potato, they became everyone's favorite lunchtime treat. Now they are in bars and restaurants everywhere, but they are even better when you make them yourself.

MAKES ABOUT 36 TOTS

4 medium (600 g) peeled potatoes

1 tbsp (7 g) organic cornstarch or potato starch

1 tsp (2 g) salt

Spray oil (*omit)

Cook the potatoes halfway, until a fork can just pierce the outside. You want them cooked but firm enough to grate. Let cool. I like to cook the potatoes the day before and grate them cold from the fridge.

Add the grated potatoes to a mixing bowl with the starch and salt. Gently toss and form into tot shapes by the tablespoon (see note below) and add to your air fryer basket. Once full, cook the first basket and form tots with the rest of the mixture.

Cook at 390°F (200°C) for 10 minutes, shake, then cook 5 minutes more. Cook the rest of the tots in shifts until they are all cooked.

NOTES: You can use a piece of perforated parchment paper under the tots to help with cleanup and make sure they don't stick.

Here's how I form the tots: Take 1 tablespoon (15 ml) of the potato mixture and put it in the palm of your hand. Place your fingers over the potato and squeeze into a tube shape. Flatten the ends, then roll it to make uniform.

AMOUNT PER SERVING: 9 tots · CALORIES: 311.5 · TOTAL FAT: 0.5 g · SODIUM: 1,230.5 mg · TOTAL CARBS: 70.5 g · DIETARY FIBER: 10.2 g · PROTEIN: 7.2 g

Indian-Inspired Veggie Tots

GLUTEN-FREE, SOY-FREE, NO OIL ADDED OPTION*

This is fusion food at its best. The wonderful flavors of an Indian appetizer are wrapped snugly inside an American favorite. Try making this a chaat by ladling on the chickpea curry and chutneys from the Samosa Chaat on page 93. These would also be great covered in a vegan creamy curry sauce!

MAKES 36 TOTS

2 cups (214 g) cauliflower florets

½ cup (54 g) grated carrot

½ cup (80 g) sliced onion

1 cup (67 g) minced kale, collards or spinach

2 tsp (12 g) grated ginger

1 tsp (3 g) minced garlic

2 tsp (4 g) garam masala

½ tsp salt

½ tsp ground cumin powder

¼ tsp ground turmeric powder

¾ cup (125 g) brown rice flour

2 tbsp (12 g) chickpea flour

2 tbsp (8 g) organic cornstarch or tapioca starch

Spray oil (*omit)

Put the cauliflower, carrot, onion, kale, ginger, garlic, garam masala, salt, cumin and turmeric into your food processor. Pulse until well mixed and in small pieces.

Add the minced veggie mixture to a mixing bowl with the chickpea flour and cornstarch. Gently toss and form into tot shapes by the tablespoon (see note below) and add to your oil-sprayed air fryer basket (or use parchment with 1-inch [2.5-cm] space around all sides to make oil-free). Once full, cook the first basket and form tots with the rest of the mixture.

Cook at 390°F (199°C) for 10 minutes, shake, then cook 2 to 3 minutes more, or until browned. Cook the rest of the tots in shifts until they are all cooked.

NOTE: Here's how I form the tots: Take 1 tablespoon (15 ml) of the mixture and put it in the palm of your hand. Place your fingers over the mixture and squeeze into a tube shape. Flatten the ends, then roll to make uniform.

AMOUNT PER SERVING: 9 tots · CALORIES: 51.3 · TOTAL FAT: 0.7 g · CHOLESTEROL: 0.0 mg · SODIUM: 317.5 mg · TOTAL CARBS: 8.7 g · DIETARY FIBER: 1.9 g · PROTEIN: 2.2 g

Battered Onion Rings

GLUTEN-FREE OPTION*, SOY-FREE, NO OIL ADDED OPTION**

I bet delicious, crunchy onion rings were first on your list to make once you bought your air fryer. They are easy to make and they get lots of crunch from the panko breadcrumbs.

> **MAKES 2 SERVINGS**

BATTER INGREDIENTS

1 cup (113 g) whole wheat flour (*use brown rice flour)

2 tbsp (14 g) organic cornstarch or tapioca starch

1 tsp (2 g) salt

½ tsp granulated garlic

½ tsp cayenne pepper (optional)

¼ tsp paprika

⅛ tsp ground black pepper

¾ cup (177 ml) vegan beer or nondairy milk

¼ cup (59 ml) aquafaba (page 22)

1 cup (62 g) panko breadcrumbs (*gluten-free)

1 large sweet onion (150 g), sliced ¼-inch (6-mm) thick and separated into rings

Spray oil (**optional)

MAKE THE BATTER

Mix the flour, starch, salt, garlic, cayenne if using, paprika and black pepper in a medium-size mixing bowl. Once combined well, add the beer and aquafaba and mix again. Add the breadcrumbs to a flat pan.

Dip a few onion rings into the batter, let the excess drain off, then press in the breadcrumbs. Layer into your air fryer basket. Repeat until your air fryer basket is about half full, alternating layers so only a couple of edges overlap.

You can add some water to your batter if it starts to thicken too much.

Spray with oil, if desired. Cook at 330°F (166°C) for 5 minutes, then cook at 370°F (188°C) for 5 minutes more, or until brown and crispy. Repeat until all the onion rings are cooked.

> **NOTE**: You can use a piece of perforated parchment paper under the onion rings to make cleanup easier and prevent sticking.

AMOUNT PER SERVING: ½ onion • CALORIES: 399.2 • TOTAL FAT: 2.6 g • SODIUM: 1,272.5 mg • TOTAL CARBS: 86.4 g • DIETARY FIBER: 10.4 g • PROTEIN: 11.5 g

Easy Sweet Potato Fries

GLUTEN-FREE, SOY-FREE, NO OIL ADDED OPTION*

Sweet potato fries are so delicious and get almost as crunchy as regular fries. The best part is they can be made quick on the spot with none of the precooking or soaking that regular potatoes need.

MAKES 4 SERVINGS

2 large sweet potatoes (450 g), peeled if not organic

2 tsp (10 ml) olive oil (*or use aquafaba [page 22])

½ tsp salt

Cut the sweet potatoes into fry shapes. I use a fry cutter if the sweet potato is fairly new and soft, but once they get hard, I can't use my model, which requires me to push it through the blade with a holder. You can just cut them as close in size as possible—rustic cuts look nice and homemade.

Toss the sweet potatoes in a bowl with oil (or aquafaba) and salt. Place one quarter to half of the fries in your air fryer basket. You don't want the basket more than half full, so this will vary depending on the size of your air fryer.

Cook at 330°F (166°C) for 10 minutes, shake and cook 5 to 10 minutes more on 370°F (188°C). They are ready when crispy outside and soft on the inside. Repeat until all the fries are cooked. (If your cuts are on the thin or thick side, your cook times may vary a bit.)

NOTE: You can use your favorite spice blend on these or even make them a sweet treat with a sprinkling of sugar and cinnamon!

AMOUNT PER SERVING: ½ of a sweet potato • CALORIES: 156.4 • TOTAL FAT: 2.6 g • SODIUM: 16.9 mg • TOTAL CARBS: 31.6 g • DIETARY FIBER: 3.9 g • PROTEIN: 2.1 g

Southern Air-Fried Hush Puppies

GLUTEN-FREE, SOY-FREE OPTION*, NO OIL ADDED OPTION**

Hush puppies are little balls of fried cornbread flecked with onions. They were originally made of a cornmeal batter that was used to coat fish. They really were given to the pups!

MAKES 24 HUSHPUPPIES

1 cup (157 g) cornmeal (fine ground if possible)

1½ tsp (5 g) baking powder

½ tsp salt

¼ cup (60 ml) soy milk mixed with 1 tsp (5 ml) apple cider vinegar (*use a different milk and omit vinegar)

¼ cup (40 g) minced onion

¼ cup (60 ml) aquafaba (page 22)

1 tbsp (12 g) vegan sugar (or sweetener of choice to taste)

1 tbsp (15 ml) olive oil (**use extra aquafaba)

Spray oil (optional)

Add the cornmeal, baking powder and salt to a medium-size mixing bowl and combine well.

Mix in the nondairy milk, onion, aquafaba, sugar and olive oil.

Scoop a tablespoon (15 g) of batter and roll into a ball. You can also just use a 1 tablespoon (15 g) scoop. Place in your air fryer basket.

Once the basket is full, spray the tops with oil if using. Bake at 390°F (200°C) for 10 minutes. Repeat until all the hush puppies are cooked.

NOTE: You can use a piece of perforated parchment paper under the hush puppies to keep them from sticking.

Buttermilk-Style Fried Pickles

GLUTEN-FREE OPTION*, SOY-FREE OPTION**, NO OIL ADDED

I never had fried pickles before I lived in New Orleans. The briny taste of pickles plus a crunchy coating, and you can count me in. Pair it with some homemade vegan ranch, and I just may need my own order!

MAKES 8 SERVINGS

2 cups (310 g) dill pickle slices

BATTER INGREDIENTS

¼ cup (28 g) whole wheat flour (*use gluten-free)

¼ cup (28 g) finely ground cornmeal

½ tsp salt

¾ cup (180 ml) soy milk plus 1 tsp (5 ml) apple cider vinegar (**use any unsweetened nondairy milk and leave out the vinegar)

2 tbsp (14 g) organic cornstarch or tapioca starch

1½ cups (120 g) whole wheat panko breadcrumbs (*use gluten-free)

Place the pickle slices in a colander over the sink while you make the batter.

MAKE THE BATTER

Mix the flour, cornmeal and salt together in a small mixing bowl. Add the curdled soy milk (or other nondairy milk) and mix again.

Place the starch in a small bowl and the breadcrumbs in another. Stab a pickle with a fork, dust it in the starch, then dip it into the batter. Let the excess batter roll off, then place in the panko, turn over and press the breadcrumbs on firmly. Place in your air fryer basket. Repeat until all the pickle slices are coated.

Cook at 400°F (205°C) for 5 minutes. If they are not quite golden brown, cook 1 or 2 minutes more. Repeat until all the pickles are cooked.

NOTE: You can use a piece of perforated parchment paper under the pickles to make cleanup easier.

AMOUNT PER SERVING: ¼ cup (60 g) • CALORIES: 163.2 • TOTAL FAT: 1.7 g • SODIUM: 1,977.6 mg • TOTAL CARBS: 32.2 g • DIETARY FIBER: 3.9 g • PROTEIN: 5.5 g

Becky Striepe's Magic Avocado Fries

GLUTEN-FREE OPTION*, SOY-FREE, NO OIL ADDED

Becky's crispy, rich avocado fries use no added oil at all. They're kind of like magic! Be sure to look for more great air fryer recipes on her blog, Glue and Glitter (www.glueandglitter.com).

MAKES 4 SERVINGS

½ cup (60 g) panko breadcrumbs (*use gluten-free panko)

½ tsp salt

Aquafaba from 1 (15-oz [427-g]) can white beans or garbanzo beans (I haven't tried with other bean liquids, but it should work just fine.)

1 Haas avocado (50 g), peeled, pitted and sliced

In a shallow bowl, toss together the panko and salt. Pour the aquafaba into another shallow bowl.

Dredge the avocado slices in the aquafaba and then in the panko, getting a nice, even coating. Arrange the slices in a single layer in your air fryer basket. The single layer is important. No overlapping, please!

Air fry for 10 minutes at 390°F (199°C), shaking well after 5 minutes.

Serve immediately with your favorite dipping sauce!

You want your avocado fries to be lightly browned and crunchy. When you do that shake after 5 minutes, take a look at the progress. They should be beginning to brown, and the panko shouldn't fall off when you shake. If your breading isn't solid after 5 minutes, keep checking once a minute before doing vigorous shaking.

NOTES: You can use a piece of perforated parchment paper under the avocado fries to make cleanup easier.

Serve these as finger food with spicy mayo for dipping or stuff them into sandwiches, tacos or burritos!

AMOUNT PER SERVING: 2 avocado slices • CALORIES: 107.2 • TOTAL FAT: 6.7 g • SATURATED FAT: 0.9 g • SODIUM: 305.6 mg • TOTAL CARBS: 10.7 g • DIETARY FIBER: 3.9 g • SUGARS: 0.1 g • PROTEIN: 2.3 g

Lime Corn on the Cob

GLUTEN-FREE, SOY-FREE, NO OIL ADDED

Ever since I had corn with lime on it, I never add vegan butter or oil to it. The lime breathes fresh life into the already flavorful fresh corn. Air frying slightly caramelizes the corn for an addictive side.

MAKES 4 SERVINGS

4 ears corn, husked and cleaned

1 lime, quartered

Salt, to taste

Optional spices like chili powder, cumin, garam masala or your favorite spice blend

Rub each ear of corn with a quarter of a lime, then sprinkle salt or your choice of seasoning over corn.

If the ears are too large to fit in your air fryer, you can cut them in half. Add 2 to 4 ears into your air fryer basket. It will vary depending on the size you have.

Cook at 400°F (205°C) for 10 minutes. Turn using tongs and cook 5 to 10 minutes more until the corn is tender.

AMOUNT PER SERVING: 1 ear of corn • CALORIES: 85.0 • TOTAL FAT: 1.0 g • SODIUM: 39.1 mg • TOTAL CARBS: 19.8 g • DIETARY FIBER: 3.5 g • SUGARS: 5.3 g • PROTEIN: 3.1 g

Southern Fried Okra

GLUTEN-FREE OPTION*, SOY-FREE, NO OIL ADDED OPTION**

Okra is an amazing vegetable and it's popular in Southern United States and Indian cooking. In the South where I'm from, we fry it like most things. In this recipe, it's dipped in nondairy milk and covered with a light coating of cornmeal and flour.

MAKES 4 SERVINGS

4 cups (400 g) sliced okra (about 16 oz [454 g]), fresh or frozen

⅔ cup (156 ml) unsweetened nondairy milk

½ cup (57 g) cornmeal

¼ cup (24 g) whole wheat pastry flour (*or use gluten-free baking mix)

1 tsp (2 g) DIY Cajun Seasoning Blend (page 65) or use store-bought

½ tsp garlic powder

½ tsp salt

¼ tsp paprika

¼ tsp cayenne pepper powder (optional)

⅛ tsp black pepper

Spray oil for cooking (**optional)

Add about 1 cup (100 g) of the okra and all the nondairy milk to a small bowl and mix.

In a larger bowl, add the cornmeal, flour, Cajun seasoning, garlic powder, salt, paprika, cayenne (if using) and black pepper. Mix well.

Use a slotted spoon and take some of the okra out of the soaking bowl, and drop them into the dry mixture. Shake or stir with a dry fork to get all parts of the okra coated with the dry mixture.

Use a dry slotted spoon and transfer the coated pieces of okra to your air fryer basket in a single layer. Repeat until your fryer basket is full.

Turn the air fryer to 390°F (200°C), add the basket full of okra, spritz some oil on top, if using, and cook for 5 minutes. Shake the basket (or use a wooden spoon if your basket is mesh), spray more oil if desired and cook 5 minutes more.

Repeat from the beginning of the instructions until all the okra has been cooked. The size of your air fryer will determine how many cooking rounds you'll need.

NOTE: Serve with your favorite vegan mayo mixed with a hot sauce like Tabasco for a dip.

AMOUNT PER SERVING: 1 cup (100 g) • CALORIES: 126.3 • TOTAL FAT: 1.7 g • SODIUM: 383.8 mg • TOTAL CARBS: 25.8 g • DIETARY FIBER: 6.4 g • SUGARS: 4.0 g • PROTEIN: 5.5 g

Salt and Pepper Baked Potatoes

GLUTEN-FREE, SOY-FREE, NO OIL ADDED OPTION*

Baked potatoes are the best when they have a crunchy skin. Adding the oil allows the salt and pepper to stick well to the outside and makes each bite perfect.

MAKES 2 SERVINGS

2 medium (426 g) russet potatoes, washed well

1–2 tsp (5–10 ml) olive oil (*or use aquafaba [page 22])

Salt and pepper

Rub each potato with oil (or aquafaba), then sprinkle with salt and pepper on all sides.

Preheat your air fryer to 390°F (199°C) unless your model doesn't require it. Once it's hot, add the potatoes to your air fryer basket.

Set the cooking time to 30 minutes. When the time is up, turn the potatoes over and cook for 30 more minutes.

Depending on the size of your potatoes, you may need to cook an additional 10 to 20 minutes. You'll know that they are ready when you can pierce them easily with a fork.

NOTES: You can use a piece of perforated parchment paper under the potatoes to make cleanup easier.

If you have a large air fryer, you can cook up to 6 medium potatoes at the same time!

AMOUNT PER SERVING: 1 potato · CALORIES: 186.8 · TOTAL FAT: 4.6 g · SODIUM: 33.9 mg · TOTAL CARBS: 33.5 g · DIETARY FIBER: 5.1 g · PROTEIN: 3.6 g

Sesame, Ginger and Garlic Edamame

GLUTEN-FREE OPTION*, NO OIL ADDED

I always get edamame when we go out and it's on the menu. I love it, but for the longest time I never made it at home. Now I always keep a few bags of whole, unshelled edamame in the freezer for a lazy meal, quick lunch or an easy cocktail snack when friends come over.

MAKES 4 SERVINGS

1 (16-oz [454-g]) bag frozen whole unshelled edamame

2 tbsp (30 ml) blood orange juice or regular orange juice

2 tbsp (30 ml) soy sauce (*or use coconut aminos)

1 tbsp (15 ml) rice wine vinegar

1 tbsp (15 ml) maple syrup or agave

1 tbsp (15 g) grated ginger

1 tsp (5 g) finely grated orange peel

½ tsp salt

Toss everything together in a bowl. Transfer the coated edamame to your air fryer basket with a slotted spoon, and save the rest of the sauce for later.

Cook on 400°F (205°C) for 5 minutes, then toss and cook 5 more minutes. The beans will begin to brown a little and should be hot.

Toss the cooked beans in the extra sauce and serve. Make sure to have empty bowls on the dinner table for the outside tough pods that you discard.

NOTES: In a large air fryer they may be done after 10 minutes, but in a smaller one, if you make the whole batch at once, it may take up to 10 additional minutes.

Try using different sauces like soy-garlic, Easy Pineapple Teriyaki Sauce (page 49) or even the Cherry Bourbon BBQ Sauce on page 108 if you feel like being a rebel!

SPECIAL DIET TIP: Believe it or not, you can make this soy-free by using coconut aminos and subbing green beans or shishito peppers for the edamame!

AMOUNT PER SERVING: 1⅓ cups • CALORIES: 104.9 •
TOTAL FAT: 2.7 g • CHOLESTEROL: 0.0 mg • SODIUM: 742.4 mg •
TOTAL CARBS: 14.1 g • DIETARY FIBER: 4.7 g • PROTEIN: 7.4 g

Stuffed Artichoke with Fresh Herbs

GLUTEN-FREE OPTION*, SOY-FREE, NO OIL ADDED OPTION**

It takes some work to prep a fresh artichoke, but it is a showstopper. We'll boil the artichoke first; then we'll stuff it and crisp it up in the air fryer. Trust me, it's worth the effort. To eat, gently pull out a leaf that's full of stuffing, and scrape your front teeth over it to get all of the stuffing and the little bits of artichoke flesh that are clinging to the leaf.

MAKES 4 APPETIZER-SIZE SERVINGS

1 large artichoke (162 g)

1 cup (112 g) panko breadcrumbs (*use gluten-free)

3 tbsp (21 g) nutritional yeast

2 tbsp (14 g) minced fresh parsley

2 tbsp (30 ml) olive oil (**or use aquafaba [page 22])

1 tbsp (7 g) minced thyme

½ tsp minced fresh rosemary

½ tsp salt

¼ tsp ground black pepper

Cut the stem of the artichoke off, making the bottom flat. Cut off the top inch (2.5 cm), and use kitchen scissors to remove the points of each of the outside leaves. Pull off any dead or damaged leaves.

Next, you are going to remove the purplish leaves in the center that you exposed when you cut the top off. These will be very tiny as you get to the bottom of them, and once they are gone, the choke will be revealed. This is the part of the artichoke you do not want to eat. Scrape it out with a spoon. Note sure what it looks like? When you scrape it, you'll see small fibers—be sure to get all of them out.

Add the prepped artichoke to a pot filled with water and bring to a boil. Lower the heat to medium-low and cover. Cook for 20 minutes.

Toss the panko, nutritional yeast, 1½ tablespoons (10.5 g) of the parsley, olive oil (or aquafaba), thyme, rosemary, salt and black pepper in a mixing bowl.

Remove the artichoke with tongs or a slotted spoon. Let cool. Transfer to a small baking dish that will fit in your air fryer. Spoon the stuffing into the middle and fill each leaf with stuffing as well.

Place the baking dish with the stuffed artichoke in your air fryer basket. Cook at 350°F (177°C) for 10 minutes, or until the stuffing is crispy and browned.

Garnish with the remaining ½ tablespoon (3.5 g) of parsley and serve.

AMOUNT PER SERVING: ¼ of the artichoke • CALORIES: 183.8 • TOTAL FAT: 7.3 g • SODIUM: 372.8 mg • TOTAL CARBS: 26.2 g • DIETARY FIBER: 4.4 g • PROTEIN: 5.9 g

Kale Brussels Sprout Spring Rolls

SOY-FREE OPTION*, NO OIL ADDED OPTION**

Everyone loves the crunch of a spring roll, and it's an awesome vehicle for healthy veggies. In this recipe, Brussels sprouts and kale are mixed in with the traditional cabbage and carrots.

MAKES 12 SPRING ROLLS

1 tbsp (15 ml) mild oil (*or water sauté)

¼ cup (40 g) minced onion

2 tsp (4 g) minced garlic

1 tbsp (6 g) grated ginger

¼ cup (60 ml) soy sauce (*use coconut aminos)

2 tbsp (30 ml) rice wine vinegar

2 tbsp (30 ml) sesame oil (**use tahini)

6–8 cups (276 g) shredded mix of kale, cabbage, carrots and Brussels sprouts

Small dish of water

12 vegan spring roll wrappers

Spray oil (optional)

Thai sweet chili sauce, for serving (optional)

NOTE: Once you make your own spring rolls, you won't ever stop. You can also use broccoli slaw, shredded cabbage and carrots for other filling shortcuts.

Heat the oil or water in a large sauté pan over medium heat. Once hot, add the onion and cook until translucent, about 5 minutes. Add the garlic and sauté a minute more. Stir in the ginger, soy sauce, vinegar and sesame oil and mix well. Add a few handfuls at a time of the kale mix, and add a few more handfuls once they cook down. Repeat until you've added all the kale mixture. Sauté until most of the sauce is cooked down and the greens are well cooked.

Set up a space to assemble your spring rolls. I use a cutting board, set a small bowl of water in the corner and fill a bowl with the cooled filling.

Place a spring roll wrapper on the cutting board with a corner pointed toward you and another pointed toward the top of the cutting board. Place 2 heaping tablespoons (30 g) of filling about 1 inch (2.5 cm) above the bottom point. Fold the point over the filling as if making a burrito. Then fold the left corner to the center, then the right to make an envelope shape. Continue rolling it up, then dip your finger in the water and wet the edges of the top corner; finish rolling and press to seal. Repeat until all the spring rolls are wrapped.

Preheat your air fryer to 390°F (200°C) unless your model doesn't require it. Once it's hot, add 4 to 6 spring rolls to your air fryer basket. If you want to, you can spritz the spring rolls with oil.

Set the cooking time to 6 minutes, and when the time is up, flip each one over with tongs. Repeat for an additional 5 minutes. If you are using oil, spritz the spring rolls with oil on the side that's facing up now. Serve with sweet chili sauce, if desired.

AMOUNT PER SERVING: 1 spring roll • CALORIES: 78.2 • TOTAL FAT: 3.6 g • SATURATED FAT: 0.5 g • SODIUM: 316.6 mg • TOTAL CARBS: 9.7 g • DIETARY FIBER: 0.9 g • SUGARS: 1.0 g • PROTEIN: 2.1 g

Garlic Breadsticks

SOY-FREE, NO OIL ADDED OPTION*

Warm homemade whole wheat breadsticks slathered with garlic spread is something I can get behind. These aren't just empty calories since the dough is made with whole grains, and there's even an oil-free option!

MAKES 8 BREADSTICKS

¼ head Roasted Garlic (page 38)

1½ tbsp (23 ml) olive oil (*or use aquafaba [page 22])

¼ tsp salt

¼ recipe Basic Whole Wheat Bread Dough (page 26), at room temperature

OPTIONAL TOPPINGS

1 tbsp (6 g) nutritional yeast

1 tbsp (9 g) poppy seeds

1 tsp (0.5 g) minced fresh rosemary

Squeeze the garlic cloves out and mash with the olive oil and salt. Roll the dough into a circle or square that fits into your air fryer, about ½ inch (12 mm) thick.

Cut a piece of parchment paper to the shape and size of the dough you have rolled out. Place it on a cutting board and place the dough on it. When I'm rolling the dough out, I keep flipping it so it doesn't stick to the cutting board.

Score the dough into 8 breadsticks by cutting halfway into the dough.

Slather the top with the garlic mixture and top with any additional topping you want to use. Place in your air fryer basket and cook at 350°F (177°C) for 10 minutes.

NOTE: Don't have time to make the garlic spread or just don't like garlic? Just drizzle some olive oil over the dough and sprinkle with salt.

AMOUNT PER SERVING: 2 breadsticks · CALORIES: 161.4 · TOTAL FAT: 2.8 g · CHOLESTEROL: 0.0 mg · SODIUM: 437.6 mg · TOTAL CARBS: 28.2 g · DIETARY FIBER: 2.3 g · PROTEIN: 4.7 g

Fried Green Olives Stuffed with Tangy Cashew Cheese

GLUTEN-FREE OPTION*, SOY-FREE, NO OIL ADDED

These little gems are full of flavor and have just the right amount of crunch on the outside. These take a little time to fill, but trust me, they are worth it. You could make a double or triple batch, freeze the extras after cooking, then heat them up in your air fryer for a last-minute treat another time.

MAKES 10 SERVINGS

½ cup (112 g) Extra-Tangy Cashew Cheese (page 37)

1 (6-oz [170-g]) can pitted green olives, drained

¼ cup (59 ml) aquafaba (page 22)

½ cup (60 g) whole wheat breadcrumbs (*use gluten-free)

Place the cashew cheese in a small resealable bag, then cut off a tiny corner, no bigger than the opening of your olives. You could also use a pastry bag with a small tip.

Fill each of the olives, then dip in aquafaba and roll in breadcrumbs. As you finish breading the olives, place them in your air fryer basket.

Cook on 400°F (205°C) for 5 minutes.

> **NOTES**: Use store-bought vegan cream cheese if you don't have the time to make your own.
>
> There will be some places that the breadcrumbs don't stick. Don't worry, they will still be delicious!

AMOUNT PER SERVING: 5 olives · CALORIES: 94.6 · TOTAL FAT: 6.9 g · SODIUM: 358.9 mg · TOTAL CARBS: 6.6 g · DIETARY FIBER: 0.8 g · PROTEIN: 1.5 g

Breakfasts

Easy and Delicious Ways to
Start Your Day

Your air fryer can make the fastest-ever breakfast sandwich, which is made extra-special with my breakfast spice blend. There's Mixed Veggie Hash (page 170), Crispy Crunchy Nutty French Toast (page 169) and even muffins and other sweets. I don't know about you, but I love to start my day with something sweet!

Quick and Easy Tofu Breakfast Sandwiches

GLUTEN-FREE OPTION*, NO OIL ADDED

I never understood why frozen breakfast sandwiches are so pricey, and they never seem to cater to vegans. You toast your English muffin or bagel in the air fryer while you cook your dry-rubbed tofu. You can even melt some vegan cheese on top if you want, or just load it with fresh veggies!

MAKES 4 SERVINGS

About 1 tsp (2 g) Breakfast Seasoning Mix (page 66)

1 (14-oz [397-g]) package extra-firm tofu, pressed and cut into 4 rectangles

4 vegan whole wheat English muffins (*or use gluten-free)

Vegan cheese slices or spread (optional)

Toppings: lettuce, tomato, avocado, cucumbers, red onion, spinach, etc.

NOTE: If you want you can cook all of the tofu at once in your air fryer and toast the English muffins in the toaster so you can serve 4 at the same time.

Rub the Breakfast Seasoning Mix on the 4 tofu rectangles. Be sure to do the front, back and edges.

If you have a large air fryer, you can cook 2 at a time; if you have a small one, you may need to do one at a time. Place 2 of the tofu rectangles in the center of the basket and place the halves of 2 English muffins on either side.

Set the temperature to 330°F (166°C) and the cooking time to 3 minutes. When the time is up, flip the tofu and the English muffin halves over. Repeat for an additional 3 minutes.

Remove the English muffins and pile on your toppings!

English muffins vary in size, so if you get small ones, you can cut the tofu in half and stack it just like the photo!

NOTE: If you want to add the sliced vegan cheese, place on tofu and cook 2 minutes more to melt. Also, you can cook the tofu a few minutes more if you prefer yours extra crispy.

AMOUNT PER SERVING: 1 breakfast sandwich · CALORIES: 321.4 · TOTAL FAT: 7.6 g · SODIUM: 736.4 mg · TOTAL CARBS: 50.3 g · DIETARY FIBER: 6.1 g · PROTEIN: 10.1 g

Crispy Crunchy Nutty French Toast

GLUTEN-FREE OPTION*, SOY-FREE, NO OIL ADDED

French toast is a perfect way to start a weekend. This recipe takes it over the top with crunchy pecans and crispy oats. You can cut the bread into fingers to make it even more fun to eat!

MAKES 4 SERVINGS

1 cup (99 g) rolled oats

1 cup (113 g) pecans, or nut of your choice

2 tbsp (12 g) ground flax seed

1 tsp (2 g) ground cinnamon

¾ cup (180 ml) nondairy milk (plain or vanilla)

8 slices whole-grain vegan bread, regular or cinnamon raisin (*use gluten-free bread)

Maple syrup, for serving

Make the topping by adding the oats, nuts, flax seed and cinnamon to your food processor and pulsing until it looks similar to breadcrumbs. Do not overblend. Pour into a shallow pan that's large enough to dip your bread slices in.

Add the nondairy milk to a second container, then soak one or two pieces of the bread for about 5 seconds, turn and soak the other side. You don't want to leave it long enough to become mushy. If your bread is fresh and moist, it may take even less time.

Place bread into your air fryer basket without overlapping. Cook at 350°F (177°C) for 3 minutes, then flip the bread and cook 3 more minutes.

Repeat until all the bread is coated and cooked.

Serve topped with maple syrup.

> **NOTES:** This makes a little over 2 cups (225 g) of topping, enough for 10 to 12 pieces of toast. If you have some left over, store it in the fridge and you can make it again the next day.
>
> Nutritionals will vary depending on the type of bread used.

NUTRITIONAL INFO (WITH DAVE'S KILLER BREAD 21 WHOLE GRAINS AND SEEDS) • AMOUNT PER SERVING: 2 slices • CALORIES: 540.1 • TOTAL FAT: 27.7 g • CHOLESTEROL: 0.0 mg • SODIUM: 374.4 mg • TOTAL CARBS: 66.6 g • DIETARY FIBER: 16.4 g • PROTEIN: 18.2 g

Mixed Veggie Hash

GLUTEN-FREE, SOY-FREE OPTION*, NO OIL ADDED OPTION**

I love all root veggies. Even turnips and radishes show their best sides once they have been roasted. In this dish, you can pick 2 root veggies to use or toss a little of all of them in. After the veggies have softened, you'll cook the tofu on top to a crispy finish.

MAKES 4 SERVINGS

2 cups (300 g) cubed potatoes (or turnips or rutabagas or a combo)

2 cups (300 g) cubed sweet potatoes (or carrots or beets or a combo)

2 tsp (10 ml) olive oil (**omit)

1 tsp (3 g) DIY Cajun Seasoning Blend (page 65 or use store-bought)

1 (15- to 20-oz [425- to 567-g]) block super-firm or high-protein tofu cut into cubes or firm tofu pressed overnight (*or use 1½ cups [360 g] cooked chickpeas)

2 tsp (4 g) Breakfast Seasoning Mix (page 66)

Toss the potatoes and sweet potatoes in a large bowl with the olive oil, if using, and the Cajun seasoning. Fill up your air fryer basket about halfway. Cook on 330°F (166°C) for 10 minutes, shake, then cook 10 minutes more.

While the veggies are cooking, toss the tofu with the Breakfast Seasoning Mix. Add on top of the veggies and cook on 390°F (200°C) for 5 minutes, then shake and cook for 5 minutes more.

Serve with a side of ketchup and some sautéed greens.

NOTE: This should all fit in an XL air fryer, but you may have to split it up and cook in 2 batches if you have a smaller one. So, you'll cook half the veggies, then half the tofu and repeat.

AMOUNT PER SERVING: 1¼ cups (405 g) · CALORIES: 281.5 · TOTAL FAT: 7.8 g · SODIUM: 302.0 mg · TOTAL CARBS: 37.5 g · DIETARY FIBER: 5.0 g · PROTEIN: 20.4 g

Cranberry Orange Muffin in a Mug

GLUTEN-FREE OPTION*, SOY-FREE, NO OIL ADDED OPTION**

Here's a quick and easy breakfast or snack recipe for you to make when everyone else is still asleep. I promise not to tell them!

MAKES 1 SERVING

¼ cup (24 g) whole wheat pastry flour (*use oat flour)

¼ tsp baking powder

Pinch salt

3 tbsp (45 ml) orange juice (or unsweetened nondairy milk plus ¼ tsp orange extract)

1 tbsp (13 g) brown or coconut sugar, or sweetener of choice to taste

2 tbsp (14 g) dried cranberries

2 tbsp (14 g) chopped nuts (optional)

1 tsp (5 ml) mild oil (**use applesauce or mashed banana)

Oil an oven-safe mug (**use a single-serving-size nonstick pan to keep it oil-free).

Add the flour, baking powder and salt, then mix well with a fork. It's important to mix well so that the baking powder is evenly distributed.

Next add the orange juice, sugar, cranberries, nuts and oil, then mix again. Bake at 350°F (177°C) for 15 minutes. Check with a fork to make sure the middle is cooked. If not, cook 5 minutes more.

AMOUNT PER SERVING: 1 mug • CALORIES: 416 • TOTAL FAT: 21.3 g • SODIUM: 124.6 mg • TOTAL CARBS: 56.1 g • DIETARY FIBER: 4.6 g • PROTEIN: 5.7 g

Banana Breakfast Muffins

GLUTEN-FREE OPTION*, SOY-FREE, NO OIL ADDED OPTION**

I bet you're asking yourself how you can make muffins in an air fryer. You can use individual silicone muffin liners or muffin cups that are made to be baked in without a muffin pan, and there are even 4-cup muffin pans that will fit in many air fryers.

MAKES 5 SERVINGS

DRY INGREDIENTS

½ cup (48 g) whole wheat pastry flour (*use gluten-free baking blend)

¼ cup (55 g) brown sugar (or sweetener of choice, to taste)

¼ cup (28 g) chopped pecans or vegan mini chocolate chips

2 tsp (4 g) ground flax seed

½ tsp cinnamon

⅛ tsp baking powder

⅛ tsp baking soda

⅛ tsp salt

Pinch nutmeg (optional)

WET INGREDIENTS

1 small banana (101 g), mashed (about ½ cup)

¼ cup (60 ml) aquafaba

2 tbsp (30 ml) mild oil (**use applesauce or extra mashed banana)

½ tsp vanilla extract

Mix the dry ingredients together in one bowl. Then mix the wet ingredients in a large measuring cup. Add the wet to the dry and mix well.

Preheat your air fryer to 350°F (177°C) (or as close as your air fryer gets).

Either spray some oil in 5 small ramekins or use individual silicone muffin cups and line with cupcake papers to keep it completely oil-free.

Place the ramekins in the fryer basket. Cook for 10 minutes. If the middle is not well set or a knife doesn't come out clean when stuck in the middle, cook for 5 minutes more.

The time may vary depending on the size ramekins and your particular air fryer.

> **NOTES:** Small ramekins are easier to find than the uber-small 4-cup muffin tray. You can also use silicone muffin holders, but I suggest using a liner to make cleanup easier.
>
> I find that my XL Philips has a dip in the basket, so I put in a grate before I add in the muffin cups to keep them level.

AMOUNT PER SERVING: 1 muffin • CALORIES: 124.2 • TOTAL FAT: 6.1 g • SODIUM: 105.0 mg • TOTAL CARBS: 20.2 g • DIETARY FIBER: 1.8 g • PROTEIN: 1.1 g

Date-Caramel Pecan Rolls

SOY-FREE, NO OIL ADDED

Once again your air fryer comes to the rescue as your second oven! This time it will quickly bake decadent yet healthy breakfast rolls for your family. These aren't your normal cinnamon rolls but instead are filled with a vegan caramel made with dates and vanilla and lots of nuts.

MAKES 8 ROLLS

²/₃ cup (115 g) chopped dates

¹/₃ cup (79 ml) water

1 tsp (5 ml) vanilla extract

¹/₈ tsp salt, optional

¼ recipe Basic Whole Wheat Bread Dough (page 26)

½ cup (55 g) chopped pecans (or a different nut of your choice or a sprinkling of chocolate chips)

NOTE: You can make these gluten-free by substituting your favorite gluten-free bread dough. One of my testers recommends using gluten-free pizza dough.

Make the date caramel by adding the dates and water to a small saucepan. Bring to a boil, then cover and remove from heat. Let sit covered until cool, then transfer to your small food processor or blender. Add the vanilla and salt and blend until smooth. If it's too thick to blend, add a tablespoon (15 ml) of water and try again.

Roll the dough out about ¼ inch (6 mm) thick in the shape of a rectangle. When I'm rolling the dough out I keep flipping it so it doesn't stick to the cutting board.

Layer two thirds of the date caramel on top, stopping ½ inch (12 mm) before the edge on 3 sides, then sprinkle the pecans on top.

Roll the dough up starting with the long side that has the caramel spread to the edge. Once rolled up, pinch the end to the main dough to seal the roll.

Cut into 8 equal pieces and place on a parchment-lined pan. I used a 2-quart (2-L) pan with a handle, but you can use any oven-safe pan that fits in your air fryer basket.

Bake at 330°F (166°C) for 10 minutes, check and cook 5 more minutes if the dough is not completely cooked in the center.

Before serving, spread the extra caramel on top.

AMOUNT PER SERVING: 1 roll · CALORIES: 162.4 ·
TOTAL FAT: 5.3 g · CHOLESTEROL: 0.0 mg · SODIUM: 182.5 mg ·
TOTAL CARBS: 25.9 g · DIETARY FIBER: 3.1 g · PROTEIN: 3.4 g

Desserts

Crispy and Baked Treats That Are Healthier Than You Think

What kind of dessert can you make in an air fryer? Think Carrot Cake in a Mug (page 183) that's thrown together in a flash after dinner, Blueberry Cake for 2 (page 180), Banana Spring Rolls (page 188) and more!

Blueberry Cake for 2

GLUTEN-FREE OPTION*, SOY-FREE OPTION**, NO OIL ADDED

One of the great things about the air fryer is that it also works like a fast-cooking convection oven. It's perfect to use on hot days when you don't want to heat up the kitchen. Use freshly picked blueberries in July or frozen ones the rest of the year to make this simple cake.

MAKES 2 SERVINGS

DRY INGREDIENTS

½ cup (48 g) whole wheat pastry flour (*or use a gluten-free baking blend)

3 tbsp (36 g) raw or coconut sugar (or sweetener of choice, to taste)

1 tbsp (12 g) ground flax seed

½ tsp baking powder

¼ tsp salt

WET INGREDIENTS

½ cup (71 g) fresh or thawed frozen blueberries

¼ cup (56 g) unsweetened vegan yogurt (**use a nut- or coconut-based yogurt)

3 tbsp (44 ml) unsweetened nondairy milk

½ tsp vanilla or lemon extract, your choice

Mix the dry ingredients together in one bowl. Then mix the wet ingredients in a large measuring cup. Add the wet to the dry and mix well.

Preheat your air fryer to 350°F (177°C) (or as close as your air fryer gets). Either spray some oil on a 5-inch (13-cm) round cake or pie pan (or a loaf pan that fits in your air fryer), or line the pan with parchment paper to keep it completely oil-free.

Place the filled pan in the fryer basket. Cook for 20 minutes. If the middle is not well set or a knife doesn't come out clean when stuck in the middle, cook for 10 minutes more. The time may vary depending on the size pan and your particular air fryer.

NOTE: If your air fryer can fit a 7-inch (18-cm) pan, you can double the recipe and have even more cake!

AMOUNT PER SERVING: ½ cake • CALORIES: 238.3 • TOTAL FAT: 2.8 g • SATURATED FAT: 1.0 g • SODIUM: 444.6 mg • POTASSIUM: 129.1 mg • TOTAL CARBS: 48.9 g • DIETARY FIBER: 6.4 g • PROTEIN: 4.1 g

Carrot Cake in a Mug

GLUTEN-FREE OPTION*, SOY-FREE, NO OIL ADDED OPTION**

Use your air fryer to make a one-serving dessert that's actually delicious. You can keep it all for yourself or make a few more mugs at the same time to share with your family. The best part is it's just like oven baked!

MAKES 1 SERVING

¼ cup (24 g) whole wheat pastry flour (*use teff flour, oat flour or a teff/oat flour mix)

1 tbsp (15 g) coconut or brown sugar, or sweetener of choice to taste

¼ tsp baking powder

¼ tsp ground cinnamon

⅛ tsp ground dried ginger

Pinch allspice

Pinch salt

2 tbsp (15 ml) plus 2 tsp (5 ml) unsweetened nondairy milk

2 tbsp (12 g) grated carrot

2 tbsp (14 g) chopped walnuts

1 tbsp (9 g) raisins or chopped dates

2 tsp (10 ml) mild oil (**use applesauce or mashed banana)

Oil an oven-safe mug (**use a single-serving-size nonstick pan to keep it oil-free).

Add the flour, sugar, baking powder, cinnamon, ginger, allspice and salt to a mixing bowl, then mix well with a fork. It's important to mix well so that the baking powder is evenly distributed.

Next add the milk, carrot, walnuts, raisins and oil, then mix again. Bake at 350°F (177°C) for 15 minutes. Check with a fork to make sure the middle is cooked. If not, cook 5 minutes more.

NOTE: Make it extra special by making the glaze on page 191 and drizzling over the top. Or take 1 tablespoon (15 g) of vegan cream cheese and whip it with 1 tablespoon (8 g) of powdered sugar to make a cream cheese topping!

AMOUNT PER SERVING: 1 mug cake without optional icing • CALORIES: 367.7 • TOTAL FAT: 20.3 g • SODIUM: 310.6 mg • TOTAL CARBS: 47.5 g • DIETARY FIBER: 6.2 g • PROTEIN: 5.6 g

Small Batch Brownies

GLUTEN-FREE OPTION*, SOY-FREE, NO OIL ADDED

Everyone loves brownies, and in our house, we love them a little too much. With that said, I've started making small batches so we can't get in trouble by eating too many. It's a bonus that the air fryer doesn't heat up your whole house like an oven does, so it's a delicious dessert to make for summer dinner parties.

MAKES 4 SERVINGS

DRY INGREDIENTS

½ cup (48 g) whole wheat pastry flour (*use gluten-free baking blend)

½ cup (99 g) vegan sugar (or sweetener of choice, to taste)

¼ cup (21 g) cocoa powder

1 tbsp (6 g) ground flax seeds

¼ tsp salt

WET INGREDIENTS

¼ cup (60 ml) nondairy milk

¼ cup (60 ml) aquafaba

½ tsp vanilla extract

MIX-INS

¼ cup (about 35 g) of any one or a combination of the following: chopped walnuts, hazelnuts, pecans, mini vegan chocolate chips, shredded coconut

Mix the dry ingredients together in one bowl. Then mix the wet ingredients in a large measuring cup. Add the wet to the dry and mix well.

Add in the mix-in(s) of your choice and mix again.

Preheat your air fryer to 350°F (177°C) (or as close as your air fryer gets). Either spray some oil on a 5-inch (13-cm) round cake or pie pan (or a loaf pan that fits in your air fryer), or line the pan with parchment paper to keep it completely oil-free.

Place the filled pan in the fryer basket. Cook for 20 minutes. If the middle is not well set or a knife doesn't come out clean when stuck in the middle, cook for 5 minutes more and repeat as needed. The time may vary depending on the size pan and your particular air fryer.

AMOUNT PER SERVING: 1 brownie • CALORIES: 225.3 • TOTAL FAT: 6.8 g • SODIUM: 157.8 mg • TOTAL CARBS: 41.0 g • DIETARY FIBER: 4.8 g • PROTEIN: 4.0 g

Grilled Peanut Butter S'mores Sandwiches

GLUTEN-FREE OPTION*, SOY-FREE, NO OIL ADDED OPTION**

Is this a dessert, a breakfast or a decadent dinner that's perfect after a stressful day at work? The decision is yours. You can make variations on this by using a different nut butter, leaving off the marshmallows or adding your favorite fruits. This recipe is freeform because you'll use more or less depending on the size of the bread slices you use, so adjust amounts accordingly.

MAKES 2 SANDWICHES

2–4 tbsp (32–64 g) peanut butter

4 slices bread (*use gluten-free)

2–4 tbsp (6–12 g) vegan mini marshmallows (or chopped large ones)

2–4 tbsp (30–60 g) vegan mini chocolate chips (**note: there is a small amount of fat in most chocolate chips)

Spray oil, optional (**omit)

Spread the peanut butter on one side of each of the 4 slices of bread. Sprinkle the marshmallows and chocolate chips over 2 of the slices, then top with the other peanut butter slices facedown.

Place one or more at a time into your air fryer depending on the size you have. You can spray the top of the sandwich if you want to use oil.

Cook 5 minutes on 330°F (166°C), then flip, spray more oil, if using, and cook 3 to 5 minutes more, until the chocolate and the marshmallows get gooey.

> **NOTE**: Depending on the size and moistness of the bread you use, you may need to cook it a little more or a little less. I find this timing works perfect for large, moist slices.

AMOUNT PER SERVING: 1 sandwich • CALORIES: 513.4 •
TOTAL FAT: 28.0 g • SATURATED FAT: 6.0 g •
POLYUNSATURATED FAT: 0.0 g • MONOUNSATURATED FAT: 0.0 g •
CHOLESTEROL: 0.0 mg • SODIUM: 225.0 mg • POTASSIUM: 0.0 mg •
TOTAL CARBS: 57.6 g • DIETARY FIBER: 6.0 g • SUGARS: 25.6 g •
PROTEIN: 18.0 g

Banana Spring Rolls

SOY-FREE, NO OIL ADDED

This is a fun dessert to have at a dinner party. They cook in no time and the filling is soft and sweet, wrapped in a crispy spring roll wrapper.

MAKES 8 SPRING ROLLS

1 medium (200 g) ripe banana

8 vegan spring roll wrappers

2–4 tsp (4–8 g) coconut sugar, or sweetener of choice to taste

Set up a space to assemble your spring rolls. I use a cutting board and set a small bowl of water in the corner. Slice the banana in half, then each half into 4 length-wise pieces (so they are in stick-like form).

Place a spring roll wrapper on the cutting board with a corner pointed toward you and another pointed toward the top of the cutting board. Place ¼ to ½ teaspoon sugar in the middle and spread it out to make a thick line, then place the banana piece on top of the sugar.

Fold the bottom point over the banana, about three fourths of the way up. Then fold the left corner to the center, then the right to make an envelope shape. Continue rolling it up, dip your finger in the water and wet the edges of the top corner, then finish rolling and press to seal.

Repeat until all the spring rolls are wrapped.

Preheat your air fryer to 390°F (199°C) unless your model doesn't require it. Once it's hot, add 4 to 8 spring rolls to your air fryer basket. If you want to, you can spritz the spring rolls with oil.

Set the cooking time to 5 minutes, and when the time is up, flip each one over with tongs. Repeat for an additional 4 minutes. If you are using oil, spritz the spring rolls with oil on the side that's facing up now.

AMOUNT PER SERVING: I spring roll · CALORIES: 50.3 ·
TOTAL FAT: 0.2 g · SODIUM: 10.2 mg · TOTAL CARBS: 11.2 g ·
DIETARY FIBER: 0.4 g · PROTEIN: 1.3 g

Mini Apple Fritters

GLUTEN-FREE OPTION*, SOY-FREE, NO OIL ADDED OPTION**

These are little bites of whole-grain and apple goodness, lightly spiced with cinnamon and allspice. You could substitute your favorite sweetener for the sugar, just adjust the batter so it's still nice and thick.

MAKES 3 DOZEN (1 TABLESPOON) MINI FRITTERS

DRY INGREDIENTS

1¹⁄₃ cups (128 g) whole wheat pastry flour (*use a gluten-free baking blend)

¹⁄₃ cup (66 g) vegan or coconut sugar

1 tsp (2 g) baking powder

½ tsp ground cinnamon

¼ tsp ground allspice

¼ tsp salt

WET INGREDIENTS

½ cup (120 ml) unsweetened nondairy milk

¾ cup (84 g) minced peeled apple

1 tbsp (6 g) ground flax seed plus 2 tbsp (30 ml) warm water

2 tsp (10 ml) mild oil (**use applesauce or pumpkin)

1 tsp (5 ml) vanilla extract

Mix the dry ingredients in a mixing bowl. Add the wet ingredients to another bowl. Add the wet to the dry and mix well.

To make cleanup easier, cut a piece of parchment paper to fit into your air fryer basket. Leave 1 inch (2.5 cm) between the parchment paper and the walls of the air fryer basket so the air can circulate freely. Or use perforated parchment paper for a bamboo steamer.

Drop 1 tablespoon (15 ml) of batter per fritter on the parchment paper. You want to leave about 1 inch (2.5 cm) between fritters or they will stick together.

Cook on 380°F (193°C) for 7 minutes; check to see if done. They will feel solid to the touch and not mash in easily. If they aren't quite done, cook 2 more minutes at a time until ready.

Repeat the process until all the fritters are cooked.

NOTE: Make a quick glaze by mixing together 2 tablespoons (14 g) of powdered sugar and 1 teaspoon (5 ml) of vanilla or water. Mix well and drizzle over your fritters!

AMOUNT PER SERVING: 1 mini fritter · CALORIES: 28.6 · TOTAL FAT: 0.5 g · SODIUM: 32.2 mg · TOTAL CARBS: 5.7 g · DIETARY FIBER: 0.7 g · PROTEIN: 0.7 g

Accessory Resources

One of the best things about an appliance like the air fryer is that you can use easy-to-find accessories to extend its uses. While you can buy air fryer specific accessories that work in your particular brand and model of air fryer, there are some you can find that are more budget-friendly.

Spray Bottles

You can buy glass or plastic spray bottles that are food safe and put your own oil, broth or aquafaba in them to spray on your food to keep it from drying out.

If you use oil, you can buy disposable spray bottles of almost any oil you'd like to use, so don't forget about them either.

Pre-Perforated Parchment

This is my favorite stuff to use in bamboo steamers and my air fryer. You can buy it on Amazon and in most Asian markets.

You can also buy parchment cake pan liners and make your own holes with a paper punch. Just fold them in quarters!

Baking Dishes

Most air fryers will fit pans between 5 and 7 inches (13 and 18 cm). Measure yours so when you go shopping, you'll know which pans to get.

You can use metal, Pyrex, silicone or any other oven-safe material. I find lots of small pie pans, mini casserole dishes and large ramekins that are new and used. I know you'll be able to find some for yours.

You can also buy brand-specific pans with handles for air fryers. If you can get them on sale or at a good price, go for it, but you can buy cheaper pans at craft stores.

Ramekins and Silicone Muffin Holders

You can get a muffin tin that makes 4 muffins at a time, but these are hard to find and not all of them fit into every air fryer. My advice is not to bother with those, and just get some silicone muffin holders because you can use them right in your air fryer basket.

Small ramekins are also great muffin makers. You can buy some new, but I always keep an eye out when I'm at thrift stores because I find them all the time and they are super cheap.

Many teacups and mugs are oven safe. Newer ones will state the fact that they are and are the best ones to try first. This is great for muffins and mug cakes!

Racks, Taco Holders and Skewers

Usually, you can buy a rack that goes with your make and model of air fryer, but they are often fairly expensive. Look for sales and keep a handy note with your air fryer measurements, because one brand of rack can be used in other air fryers as long as it's compatible in size.

Racks can be used to cook 2 layers of food, like veggie burgers over fries. They can also help hold down tortillas. Some racks come with mini skewers, and that's a fun way to make vegan kabobs. You can use wooden kebob sticks and cook right in the basket as long as you can find a size small enough to fit in your air fryer.

You can also buy little metal taco holders to make crispy tacos in your air fryer. I suggest pinning the tops together with toothpicks to keep them from blowing open.

Online Resources

I'm not the first air-frying vegan. There's a huge community out there, especially in Facebook groups.

MY PRIVATE FACEBOOK GROUP WHERE YOU CAN ASK ABOUT VEGAN COOKING IN GENERAL:
www.facebook.com/groups/VeganCookingWithKathy

JL FIELDS'S VEGAN AIR FRYING FACEBOOK GROUP:
www.facebook.com/groups/TheVeganAirFryer

SUSAN VOISIN'S FATFREE VEGAN AIR FRYERS FACEBOOK GROUP:
www.facebook.com/groups/FatFreeVeganAF

You should also do a search for the make of your air fryer and see if it has a page or group on Facebook. These probably won't be vegan groups, but you might find out more tips and tricks specific to your model.

Acknowledgments

This is my fourth book with Page Street Publishing and I adore working with Will Kiester, Marissa Giambelluca and their supportive team, including my developmental editor, Karen Levy, who was particularly helpful!

Lisa and Sally Ekus are the best agents ever and wonderful friends, too. Plus Sally is the reason I wrote an air fryer book at all.

I have so much gratitude for my testers' help, patience and guidance: Brandie Faust, Michelle L. Imber, Sherrie Thompson, Amy Katz, Dianne Wenz, Jennifer Murphy, Kim Logan, Rochelle Arvizo, Maureen Johnson, Cathy Cintolo, Sandra Ryan, S. Hancock, Sherene Silverberg, Mary Baker, Dawn Meisch and Robert Meisch.

I love Meg Baskis and Laura Gallant's wonderful layout and book design, and thank them for all their patience and hard work. As usual, I can't possibly thank Cheryl Purser enough for cleaning up the kitchen a bazillion times while I wrote this book.

About the Author

Kathy Hester is the author of *The Ultimate Vegan Cookbook for Your Instant Pot, The Easy Vegan Cookbook, The Great Vegan Bean Book* and the best-selling *The Vegan Slow Cooker*. She's the blogger behind HealthySlowCooking.com; does freelance writing, food styling, food photography and recipe development; and teaches people just how easy it is to cook.

When she's not writing or being a mad scientist in the kitchen, she's probably drinking tea on the deck while reading Harry Potter one more time. She lives in Durham, North Carolina, with a grown-up picky eater, two quirky dogs and one grumpy cat.

Index